THE REVOLUTIONARY YEARS, 1775-1789

Related Titles from Potomac Books

THE REVOLUTIONARY YEARS, 1775-1789

The Art of American Power During the Early Republic

WILLIAM NESTER

Potomac Books
Washington, D.C.

Maps by Chad Blevins

ISBN 978-1-59797-674-9

Printed in the United States of America

Potomac Books, Inc.
22841 Quicksilver Drive
Dulles, Virginia 20166

Book Club Edition

Contents

Maps

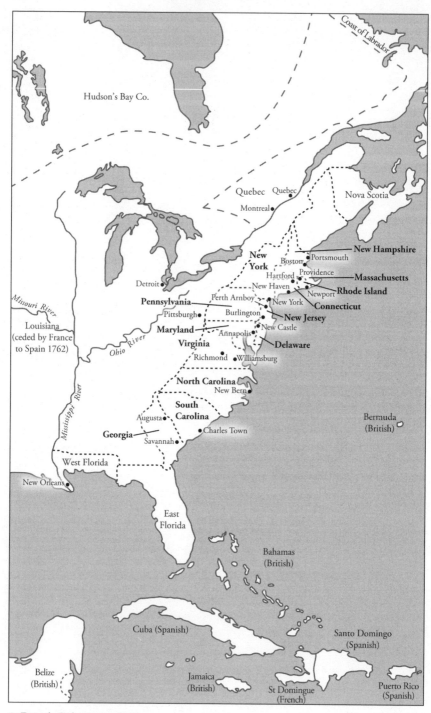

1. **British Colonies in 1763**

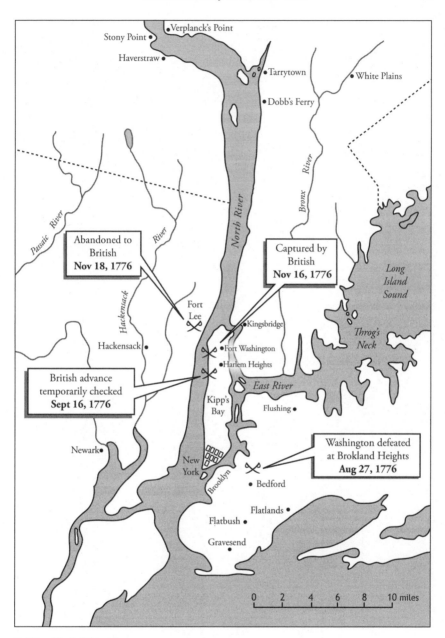

2. New York Campaigns

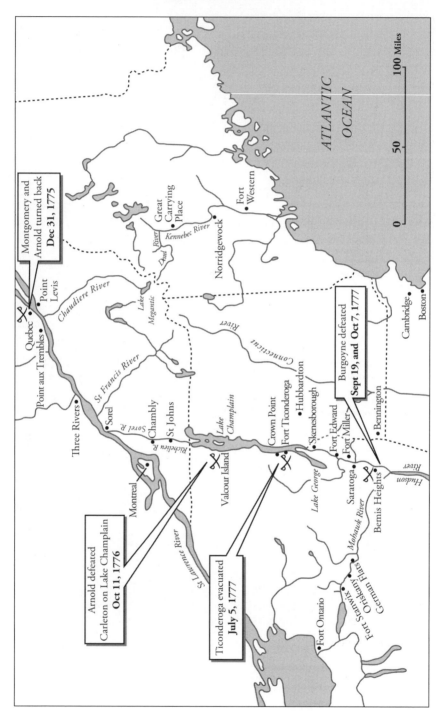

3. Campaigns in the North

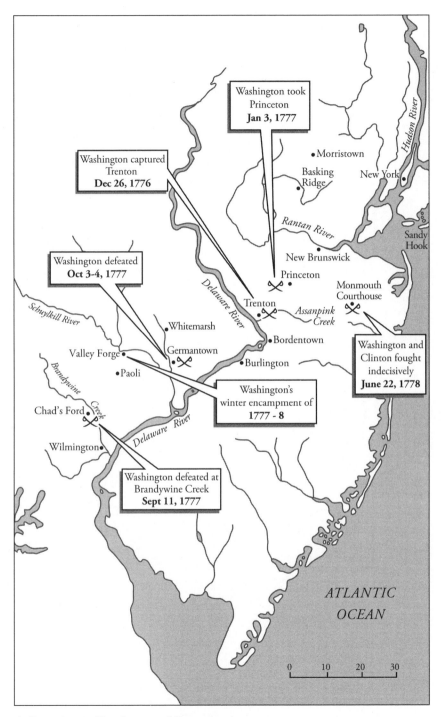

4. Campaigns in New Jersey and Pennsylvania

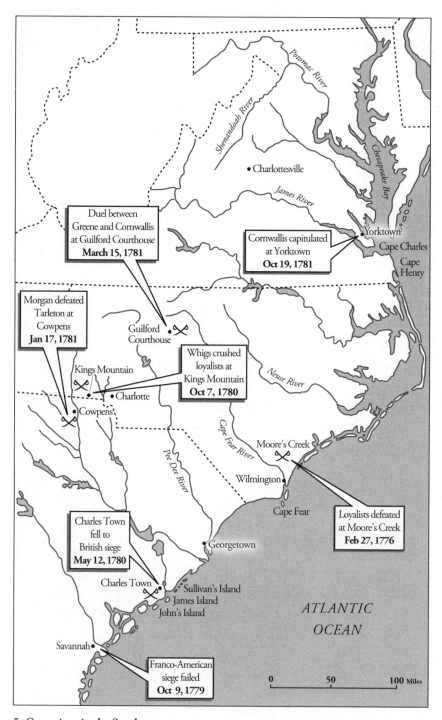

Duel between
Greene and Cornwallis
at Guilford Courthouse
March 15, 1781

Cornwallis capitulated
at Yorktown
Oct 19, 1781

Morgan defeated
Tarleton at
Cowpens
Jan 17, 1781

Whigs crushed
loyalists at
Kings Mountain
Oct 7, 1780

Charles Town
fell to
British siege
May 12, 1780

Loyalists defeated
at Moore's Creek
Feb 27, 1776

Franco-American
siege failed
Oct 9, 1779

Charlottesville

Potomac River

Shenandoah River

James River

Chesapeake Bay

Yorktown
Cape Charles
Cape
Henry

Guilford
Courthouse

Neuse River

Kings Mountain
Charlotte

Cowpens

Pee Dee River

Cape Fear River

Moore's Creek
Wilmington

Cape Fear

Georgetown

Charles Town
Sullivan's Island
James Island
John's Island

*ATLANTIC
OCEAN*

Savannah

0   50   100 Miles

5. Campaigns in the South

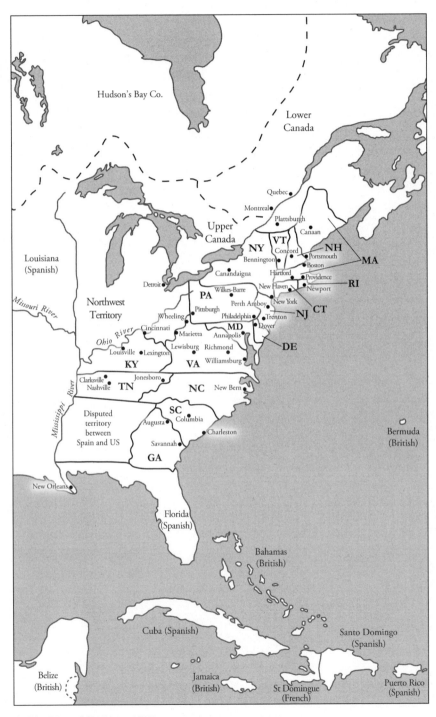

6. The United States in 1789

Acknowledgments

I cannot express enough my deep gratitude to Elizabeth Demers, senior editor at Potomac Books, first for wanting to publish my Art of American Power series and then for carefully editing each book. She made numerous corrections and wonderful suggestions that greatly strengthened my books. She is an outstanding professional in her field. I also want to thank Kathryn Neubauer for her own wonderful editing of my manuscript.

Introduction
Nation-Building, Revolution, and the Art of Power

*It is a maxim founded on the universal experience of mankind that
no nation can be trusted farther than it is bound by its interest,
and no prudent statesman or politician will venture to depart from it.*
GEORGE WASHINGTON

*We should be as independent on the charity of our friends,
as on the mercy of our enemies.*
JOHN JAY

*It is obvious that all the powers of Europe will be continually maneuvering with us,
to work us into their real or imaginary balances of power.*
JOHN ADAMS

*I have ever considered diplomacy as the pest of the peace of the world,
as the workshop in which nearly all the wars of Europe are manufactured.*
THOMAS JEFFERSON

I am not a Virginian, but an American.
PATRICK HENRY

If the United States ever had a "greatest generation," then surely it was the first.[1] The Founders won American independence and crafted and implemented a liberal democratic political system that has not only endured for more than two centuries but has evolved in ways that have come ever closer to realizing the ideals that inspired it. All that would have been impossible had the Founders not mastered the art of power.

Americans celebrate George Washington as a great leader in war and peace but tend to slight him as a thinker. Yet his thousands of letters and journal pages are filled with sound insights into the problems of his day and beyond. In one such missive, he succinctly defined the ground in which to root a nation's foreign policies: "It is a maxim founded on the universal experience of mankind that no nation can be trusted farther than it is bound by its interests, and no prudent statesman or politician will venture to depart from it."[2]

Washington understood perfectly but left unsaid that power was the crucial link between interests and policies. The art of power boils down to three dynamics: getting others to do something they otherwise would not do, getting others not to do something they otherwise would do, and taking from others what they would otherwise keep. Yet no matter what one is striving to achieve, power must be wielded in a way that maintains and ideally begets more power. That demands a careful calculation of ends and means. Those who get what they want are relatively powerful, even if their aims are modest; those whose ambitions exceed their abilities are relatively powerless.[3]

America's leaders during the early-republic era struggled to find the means to assert the nation's related economic and strategic interests. They saw themselves beset by foes in a harsh Hobbesian world. As John Jay put it, "We shall always be deceived if we believe that any nation in the world has, or will have, a disinterested regard for us." Thus, Americans "should be as independent on the charity of our friends, as on the mercy of our enemies." Jay was hardly alone in his bleak assessment. John Adams echoed his colleague's view of the dangers facing the new republic: "It is obvious that all the powers of Europe will be continually maneuvering with us, to work us into their real or imaginary balances of power."[4]

Clearly, the best strategy was to play off the great powers against one another. That timeless strategy—"the enemy of my enemy is my friend"—was a given and would be vigorously applied in the decades to come. Yet on top of that, Americans enjoyed special circumstances that could help make up for their economic and military deficiencies if they recognized and acted on them. Here again, George Washington identified enduring principles to guide American foreign policy. His farewell address of 1796 called on Americans to best ensure the nation's peace and prosperity by trading with all and permanently allying with none.[5] More specifically, Americans should take full advantage of their vast and expanding territory and population, the distance from Europe, and the perennial conflicts among Europe's great powers. But Washington understood that those advantages would not always be enough. At times, sabers had to be rattled and troops had to be marched to the brink of war, either to deter aggression or to compel submission. And on extremely rare occasions, when all else had failed, the nation itself must wage war.

Washington's Herculean challenges as, first, the commanding general during the independence war and then as the first president under the Constitution were continually undermined by the nation's deficiencies in "hard" power—most notably men, arms, money, and organization. That made all the more crucial the ability to mobilize and wield power's "soft" side—leadership, diplomacy, conviction, morale, teamwork, and devotion. He saw in himself only one essential strength: "a firm belief in the justice of our Cause—close attention to the prosecution of it—and the strictest integrity—If these cannot supply the places of Ability & Experience, the Cause will suffer & more than probably my character along with it, as reputation derives its principal support from success." Yet while Washington was confident in his own unshakable character and commitment, he could not vouch for that of anyone else. Although he lauded all "the talk of patriotism," he recognized that "whoever builds upon it, as a sufficient basis for conducting a long and bloody War, will find themselves deceived in the end. . . . For a time it may . . . push men to action. . . . but it will not endure unassisted by interest."[6] In these two letters, Washington reveals brilliant insights into the nature of soft power expressed by the vital importance of integrity, patriotism, and, above all, self-interest. Time after time, as he fought for independence and later when he served as president, his ability to mobilize and wield soft power often made up for otherwise crippling shortfalls of hard power in asserting American interests.

The art of power is the ability to get what one wants. What one wants, however, can change with time. Nearly all of those who struggled against British misrule before 1776 wanted reform, not revolution, and autonomy, not independence. Only after the king and Parliament declared the colonies to be in a state of rebellion and refused any compromise did those who led the reform movement embrace outright independence. There was just as sharp a shift in how Americans sought to govern themselves. Although the Founders were committed to republican ideals of equal rights and representation, most at first favored a confederation of sovereign states. Only after that proved to be unworkable did a majority advocate a sovereign federation of autonomous states.

To prevail in those struggles, the Americans had to muster and eventually command two powerful historic forces—nationalism and liberalism. From 1775 to 1783, they wielded those forces to defeat the world's most professional army and mightiest navy. Hot lead and cold steel ultimately determined American independence. The Americans lost more battles than they won, but their ability to stay in the fight, repeatedly square off with the British, and capture enemy armies at Saratoga and Yorktown finally shattered the resolve of the king and Parliament. The Americans, however, could not have won independence when and how they did without massive French military and financial aid. That in turn depended on American victories in the field and the persistent art of diplomacy, among the more crucial dimensions of power, wielded by Benjamin Franklin and his colleagues in Paris.

Military and diplomatic battles, however, were relatively infrequent during the leisurely pace of eighteenth-century warfare. Political battles, on the other hand, were incessant. Within and beyond Congress, the Founders disputed just what the liberty and the equality they had declared independence for meant, whether they complemented or conflicted with each other, and how they were best defended. With independence won, a related but far less abstract debate erupted. Would the United States be thirteen sovereign states or one nation? Those who advocated the United States of America triumphed during the sweltering, seemingly endless months in Philadelphia from May to September 1787, when the delegates hammered out the Constitution. The art of power it took to draft and ratify the Constitution was grounded in the deft political skills of cutting deals and manipulating public opinion.

Although with the Constitution's ratification the Revolution came to a symbolic and substantive end, ever since then Americans have debated and at times shed blood, most tragically during the Civil War, over just what the Founders intended and just how to realize those ideals.

Building a nation and the government to run it are among the most daunting of challenges. There is somewhat of a chicken-and-egg dilemma to creating a modern nation-state. Ideally, the characteristics of the nation and the state at once reflect and shape each other.

During the eighteenth century's second half, America was a nation whose people were in search of a legitimate government. America had been developing as a nation for more than a century and a half before its leaders were able to achieve independence and devise an enduring political system.[7] In crucial ways the development of national power depended on creating institutions, laws, and policies that exemplified American values and interests. The text of the Declaration of

Independence best expressed the "American mind"; that of the Constitution provided the institutions that would best express that American mind.

That emerging American mind was reflected and shaped by some defining documents and events—the Mayflower Compact (1620), by which the colonists created their own self-governing community; John Smith's "General History of Virginia" (1624), which spoke of the opportunity and the freedom available in the New World; John Winthrop's "City on a Hill" sermon (1635), which described the Puritan communities in Massachusetts as a beacon of hope and salvation for all peoples everywhere; the heresy trial transcripts (1637) of the dissident Anne Hutchinson; "The Bloody Tenet of Persecution for Cause of Conscience" (1644) of Roger Williams, who sought religious freedom; the charters of Connecticut (1662) and Rhode Island (1663), by which the king let the citizens of those colonies choose their own governors; William Penn's charter (1693), enshrining religious toleration for what would become Pennsylvania; the founding of the colleges of Harvard (1636) and William and Mary (1693); Anne Bradstreet's books of poetry (1650, 1678), celebrating love and nature; Cotton Mather's sermons and "Magnalia" (1702), extolling hard work, enterprise, family, and deferred gratification as the road to salvation; William Byrd's "History of the Dividing Line" (1728), expressing the joys of exploring the wilderness; the John Zenger trial, which promoted freedom of the press (1735); and Benjamin Franklin's founding of the American Philosophical Society (1743), the practical advice of his *Almanac* (1732–58), and his attempt to unite the colonies with his "Plan of Union" (1754).

The development of American liberalism and nationalism was not all homegrown. Americans were not merely children of the Enlightenment; they ultimately fulfilled its ideals with their own revolution. Learned men avidly read and tried to apply the liberal political philosophy expressed by the spectrum of Enlightenment writers, especially John Locke and Charles de Secondat, the baron Montesquieu. They were also steeped in the classical works of Aristotle, Cicero, Tacitus, Livy, and Plutarch, who taught them that republican institutions were only as strong as the virtues of the men who ran them. In addition, they absorbed the lessons learned from such critical events in the mother country as the Petition of Rights by Parliament to Charles I (1628), the overthrow of the monarchy by Parliament and the ensuing Commonwealth (1642–60), and the Glorious Revolution (1688–89), which included a Declaration of Rights and parliamentary supremacy.

Yet it was the tough school of worldly experience that provided the most important lessons of all. The colonists suffered continual reminders of their secondary status and economic restrictions within the British Empire. The Navigation Acts forced the Americans to trade only with or through England and prevented them from producing a lengthening list of goods. Political autonomy compensated somewhat for economic dependence. Ever more democratic institutions developed that at once safeguarded and were nurtured by the deepening democratic values. Each colony had a representative assembly, although who was eligible to vote or run for office varied. Americans honed their political skills in nearly constant conflicts among themselves and with the governors sent over by the king.

War was the most powerful catalyst for transforming English colonists into Americans.[8] The threat from Indians, the French, and Spaniards was near, while help from the mother country was far away. Although the king usually sent troops and warships in times of war, the Americans mostly had to rely on themselves. It was up to each colony, either alone or together as circumstances demanded, to organize, arm, supply, and march troops against their enemies.

The alliance of the French and their Indian allies was the worst threat to the colonies. In all, the American colonists fought five wars against the French Empire—the Huguenot War (1628–32), the King William's or League of Augsburg War (1689–97), the Queen Anne's or Spanish Succession War (1701–13), the King George's or Austrian Succession War (1740–48), and the French and Indian or Seven Years' War (1754–63). Although the frontier settlements bore the brunt of the raids, each colony mobilized taxes and troops from across its realm to thwart those attacks.

That last war dwarfed all of those that preceded it in scale, casualties, and, most important, goals.[9] It was fought not only in North America, but across much of Europe and the Caribbean and in parts of West Africa, India, Argentina, and the Philippines, and the seas linking those distant lands. It eventually engulfed the other great powers of Prussia, Austria, Spain, and Sweden, along with a host of minor realms.

The first shots in that war were ordered by none other than George Washington, who was then a twenty-three-year-old lieutenant colonel of the Virginia militia, as well as a land speculator in the Ohio River Valley frontier. His troops ambushed a French patrol in disputed territory near the forks of the Ohio River on May 27, 1754. That deadly attack sparked what would become the first global war.

This time the British crown sought to conquer, rather than merely contain, the neighboring French Empire. Under the 1763 Treaty of Paris, the French and their ally Spain ceded all their mainland possessions east of the Mississippi and south of the Arctic Circle to Britain. The French threat to the Americans had vanished forever, but soon a new threat emerged to take its place.

The French and Indian War and its aftermath completed the transformation of colonists into Americans. The North American campaigns were decisive for

British victory, and American soldiers were an essential component of nearly every campaign, either in marching with British regulars or in defeating the French and the Indians on their own.

Yet the British were anything but grateful for that contribution. They lost no chance to sneer at and snub their American counterparts, denigrating their military prowess and dismissing their victories. Policy codified those attitudes. An American officer was always treated as if he were a rank lower than his designated rank when he stood alongside a British officer of equal rank. George Washington was only one of tens of thousands of his countrymen who bristled at the British snobbery and attempts to hog the glory of victory. They knew what sacrifices they had made and what feats of arms they had performed. Yet it was hardly hurt feelings alone that led to the American Revolution.

The British government, known as Whitehall after the complex of buildings in London where it was housed, trapped itself in an ultimately self-destructive dilemma. It feared that the Americans' growing autonomy and identity would eventually lead to outright independence. So to prevent that, Whitehall kept thousands of troops in the colonies and imposed a series of taxes and other restrictions. That enraged, rather than cowed, the Americans. They protested that Whitehall was violating two of their fundamental rights as British subjects: taxes were imposed on them, even though they had no representatives in Parliament to defend their interests, and those taxes were enforced by a standing army of redcoats in their midst. The policies that were intended to crush American independence actually promoted it.

For Whitehall, of course, the key issue was not violated rights but the Americans' ingratitude for British military protection and an unwillingness to pay their fair share for that privilege. There was no question that the British crown needed the money—the national debt had soared from 72 million pounds sterling in 1754 to 146 million pounds sterling in 1763 during the French and Indian War. But an irony was lost on most of those ministers who devised and enacted policy. The cost of keeping troops in the colonies to enforce a series of taxes far exceeded the revenues they produced. The Stamp Act of 1765 was the most ambitious. It imposed a tax not only on all official documents, such as mercantile, land, or marriage contracts, but on such items as liquor, newspapers, pamphlets, playing cards, and dice. Because virtually no one could escape paying one or more of those taxes, almost everyone was angered.

As if the Stamp Act were not onerous enough, it was imposed on top of other Whitehall measures viewed as offensive by most Americans during the preceding two years. The Proclamation of 1763 forbade any American settlements west of the Appalachian Mountains. The policy was designed to prevent Americans from provoking wars with the Indians by taking their lands, but Americans condemned the proclamation as a violation of both the right and the need of a swelling population to claim and settle wilderness ever farther west. The Sugar Act of 1764 actually reduced the tax from six to three pence a gallon to undercut smugglers but required smuggling trials to be conducted at faraway Halifax in Nova Scotia, rather than before a jury of peers in the home port. The Quartering Act of 1765 required towns to provide barracks, firewood, candles, salt, beer, and rum to the British soldiers deployed in their midst.

From 1765 to 1775, Americans expressed their swelling anger mostly in the form of protests, petitions, boycotts of British goods, and the mass publication of hundreds of pamphlets that mixed reason and emotion in promoting their cause. Committees of Correspondence were set up to coordinate resistance among the colonies. The first significant unified assertion of American interests was the Stamp Act Congress of 1765, which met in New York City and included twenty-seven delegates from nine colonies. But the political dissent was increasingly peppered with sporadic violence. Mobs, often provoked by the radical Sons of Liberty, a group that believed that Whitehall would yield only to force, tarred and feathered officials and outspoken Tories, broke windows or outright torched their homes, and brawled with British soldiers and sailors.

That opening barrage of resistance was effective. The king and Parliament conceded by revoking the Stamp Act in 1766. But in 1767, King George III tried to reassert his government's authority with the Declaratory Act, which proclaimed parliamentary supremacy over the colonies, and the Townshend Act of new taxes, this time on paper, lead, glass, paint, and tea. That provoked a new round of protests and violence. Once again, the British government eventually conceded by withdrawing a hated tax but replaced it with a lighter one to assert its authority. In 1770 all items on the list of taxable goods were revoked except tea. Protests flared briefly, then smoldered.

For the next three years, the king and Parliament did nothing new to provoke Americans' sensitivities. Yet they retained the essential absurdity of their policies. Redcoats remained in New York, Boston, and a few smaller posts, ostensibly to keep order and remind the Americans of their subjection to the monarchy. Meanwhile, the tea tax paid for no more than a pittance of the army's upkeep; the burden fell on the communities in which the troops were quartered.

Tensions between government officials and soldiers, on one hand, and the Americans, on the other, at times erupted into sporadic violence. The most spectacular act was the American capture and burning of the HMS *Gaspee*, a revenue schooner that ran aground in Narragansett Bay in 1772. Then in early 1773, riots resulted in two American deaths in New York and seven in Boston; American propagandists condemned those deaths as "massacres."

That same year Whitehall committed its latest blunder. The Tea Act of 1773 actually reduced the tax on tea. Like the Sugar Act of 1764, the intention was to undercut smugglers. The trouble was that the Tea Act also gave a monopoly over tea sales to the nearly bankrupt East India Company. In doing so, the crown deprived all those tea merchants not affiliated with the crown's favorite. Those who urged all Americans to boycott tea redoubled their efforts. In December 1773 three East Indian ships with loads of tea lay anchored in Boston harbor. A horde of "patriots" swarmed aboard those vessels and dumped their cargo of tea into the sea.

That violence was highly effective in a way that complemented the nonviolent efforts. The Boston Tea Party provoked Whitehall into imposing four harsh measures known as the Intolerable or Coercive Acts of 1774 that in turn radicalized ever more Americans. The Boston Port Act cut off the city's trade until it paid for the destroyed tea; to enforce that policy, more than four thousand redcoats blanketed the city, a fleet was anchored in the harbor, and Gen. Thomas Gage was appointed the governor. The Massachusetts Government Act revoked parts of the charter and empowered Gage to dismiss the assembly and pack the council with his own men. A revised Administration of Justice Act took away the power of colonial prosecutors to put on trial and juries to judge any British soldier or official accused of crimes. The Quartering Act allowed governors to appropriate public buildings for troops if colonial assemblies refused to allocate them, although not private homes, as is popularly believed. That same year, Parliament passed the Quebec Act, which extended that colony's territory south to the Ohio River, thus trumping the conflicting claims of Virginia, Pennsylvania, New York, and Connecticut to that land and shutting off that territory to American hunters, traders, and settlers.

Whitehall thus sought to make a harsh example of Massachusetts and intimidate the rest of the colonies into compliance. Instead, it made a martyr of that colony, especially occupied Boston, and inspired greater solidarity among Americans against what they believed was a tyrannical government that was violating their rights and liberties.

The result was the convening in Philadelphia on September 5, 1774, of the First Continental Congress, which included fifty-six delegates from all thirteen colonies. The delegates initiated what would become a perennial debate among Americans over just how best to govern themselves. Benjamin Franklin introduced plans for a union of the colonies into a permanent congress and proportional representation in Parliament; those steps were still too radical for a majority of the delegates and were not approved. Having agreed to disagree on those is-sues, they then succeeded in finding common ground elsewhere. They resolved to demand that Parliament revoke all of its Intolerable Acts and backed that up with an agreement not to import any goods from Britain. They sent a petition to King George asking him to intercede in their favor against Parliament. They adjourned on October 26, with the intention of meeting again for a Second Continental Congress on May 10, 1775.

The achievements of the First Continental Congress were revolutionary. Yet perhaps the single most important symbolic event came in the midst of a stirring speech by Patrick Henry, in which he declared, "I am not a Virginian, but an American."

PART 1

The American Revolution, 1775–1781

If we do not hang together, we will most assuredly all hang separately.
BENJAMIN FRANKLIN

The United States was destined beyond a doubt to be the greatest power on earth, and that within the life of man.
JOHN ADAMS

[The French] are interested in separating us from Great Britain and on that point we may, I believe, depend upon them; but it is not their interest that we become a great and formidable people, and therefore they will not help us to become so.
JOHN JAY

We hold these truths to be self-evident, that all men are created equal and endowed by their Creator with certain inalienable rights; that among these are life, liberty, and the pursuit of happiness.
DECLARATION OF INDEPENDENCE

1

From Lexington Green to Bunker Hill

Gen. Thomas Gage faced a terrible dilemma.[1] The king had given him sweeping powers to accomplish what appeared to be a mission impossible. As both the commander-in-chief of British forces in North America and the governor of Massachusetts, he was empowered to crush all those who defied the king's will. Yet Whitehall's harsh laws and policies backed by ever more soldiers and warships had provoked more rather than less resistance. Militia companies were stockpiling arms, munitions, and supplies at key towns throughout the region. Committees of Public Safety had formed to supersede local governments; they coordinated policies and exchanged information through Committees of Correspondence. Barred from their own assembly, most of Massachusetts' legislators had illegally convened a Provincial Congress in Concord, a score of miles west of Boston; it was rumored that a large magazine including cannons was hidden there. In Philadelphia a congress of all the colonies had met and passed a set of resolutions and petitions that promoted the American cause, and then adjourned but would reconvene in May.

Gage had sent expeditions to seize military supplies at Portsmouth in December 1774 and Salem in January 1775. Both were humiliating failures. At Portsmouth the militia managed to spirit away most of the supplies before the redcoats arrived and then jeer at them until they departed. Even worse was the British experience on the road to Salem; the militia merely raised a drawbridge across a swollen creek, leaving the British commander to sputter demands and curses in impotent rage at the taunting colonials before marching his troops back to Boston.

Gage was determined that a third expedition would not fail.[2] He secretly organized a force of nine hundred troops, which included two regular regiments and a provisional battalion composed of the elite grenadier and light infantry companies from the other regiments. The plan was for Lt. Col. Francis Smith to quick-march this force from Boston westward during the night of April 18, get to Concord around dawn on April 19, and seize the rebel leaders and the magazine.

Spies learned about the expedition and its route. Riders, including Paul Revere, galloped through the dark night, warning of the approaching British column. The Americans were well organized. Each town had both a militia company and a Committee of Correspondence. As a town's troops mustered, new riders carried word across the region. By sunrise, scores of companies were marching toward Concord or its road to Boston.

The head of the British column reached Lexington just before dawn. The town's militia company was waiting silently, nervously on the green. Maj. John Pitcairn deployed his troops and demanded that the militia disperse. A few men slipped away, but most stood firm. Someone fired a shot. Then the redcoats fired a volley, killing ten and wounding nine. The militia scattered, and the redcoats marched on.

Hundreds of militia had gathered at Concord but withdrew from the town as the British column approached. Smith had some of his troops search the buildings, and he detached companies to guard the roads converging on the town. The redcoats found little. The rebel leaders and most of the supplies had long before reached safety. Smith ordered a bonfire made of the few provisions his troops had gathered.

As black smoke rose from Concord's center, the militia feared that the redcoats were torching the entire town. Those beyond the North Bridge advanced toward the British detachment; volleys were exchanged, and the regulars broke and ran. As those troops streamed back into town, Smith ordered his troops to withdraw to Boston.

The battle had only begun. The Americans hounded the British nearly all the way back to Boston. Ever more companies from the surrounding countryside joined the pursuit. They might have killed or captured Smith's entire command had not a second column of 900 troops arrived and driven them off. In all, Gage had committed nearly half of his 3,800 troops to this expedition and lost 73 killed and more than 200 wounded to the 49 dead and 41 wounded Americans.[3] The British had suffered a humiliating defeat.

Gage and his troops holed up in Boston and prepared for a siege. Ever more militia companies from Massachusetts and neighboring colonies swelled the ranks of the provincial army camped in three divisions around the city. In all, Gen.

Artemas Ward commanded around fifteen thousand colonials. Within little more than a week, committees of correspondence had relayed word of that first stunning American victory to the far corners of the colonies.

Those first intoxicating triumphs briefly diverted the Americans from the fact that they faced overwhelming odds. In April 1775 the British had over 7,000 troops in the colonies, with nearly 4,000 in Boston and another 20,000 in the home islands and elsewhere. Britain's navy was the world's largest, with more than a hundred warships. More than 8 million people lived in the British Isles. Britain had the world's most advanced economy. London was the world's financial capital. The industrial revolution was already well underway, fueled by related agrarian, mercantile, scientific, technological, and financial revolutions. Even then the sun did not set long on British power. Beyond North America, there were colonies in Gibraltar and Minorca, half a dozen Caribbean islands with Jamaica the crown jewel, Senegal and Gambia in West Africa, and Bombay and Bengal in India. As an island nation, the British enjoyed a vast moat which at once encouraged seafaring and trading but kept enemies at bay.

King George III was then a vigorous forty-six years old and a couple of decades away from the illness that would manifest as his "madness." Six ministers comprised the cabinet, with Frederick, Lord North, the king's chief minister. The American war would mostly be run by George, Lord Germain, the secretary of state for the Southern Department. The king, his cabinet, and most members of Parliament were united behind the policy of decisively crushing the rebellion and reasserting the crown's rightful rule over the colonies.

Nonplused by the odds against them, the Americans would shift their goals from conciliation and reform to independence and revolution during the fourteen months after Lexington and Concord. The success of that revolution would depend on the power of American resolve, arms, diplomacy, luck, and, above all, leadership.

Among America's war leaders, no one surpassed and few matched Benedict Arnold in courage, charisma, vision, and skill.[4] In April 1775 he was among the militia captains who led his men into the camps around Boston. Not content to sit tight and wait for something to happen, he talked Gen. Israel Putnam, who commanded Connecticut's troops, into granting him a commission to gather volunteers and capture the British forts of Ticonderoga and Crown Point on Lake Champlain on New York's far northern frontier. Taking those lightly manned forts would greatly boost the American cause—they were packed with cannons, munitions, and provisions that were desperately needed by the army besieging Boston; they also guarded the easiest route to and from Canada.

Arnold was not alone in recognizing the importance of those forts.

Col. Samuel Parsons had independently received permission to lead his troops on the same mission. Then there was Ethan Allen, the boisterous and flamboyant commander of the Green Mountain Boys, the militia in what is now Vermont. The Green Mountain Boys rejected the conflicting claims of New York and New Hampshire for the territory and demanded that Vermonters be allowed to govern themselves. Upon reaching Bennington, Parsons agreed to subordinate his command to Allen. Arnold caught up with them at Castleton and presented his commission to Allen. After a tense confrontation, they agreed to jointly command the three hundred–man expedition. Without firing a shot, they took Fort Ticonderoga on May 9 and Crown Point the next day; unaware that fighting had broken out, the startled commanders surrendered their garrisons. The Americans seized over a hundred cannons along with dozens of bateaux and a sloop. Arnold sailed north down Lake Champlain with about forty men aboard the sloop and captured St. John's with its supplies and an armed sloop. Rather than try to hold St. John's, Arnold had the supplies packed aboard the vessels and sailed back to Ticonderoga.

Meanwhile the siege of Boston continued. Except for spies, nearly all those Bostonians sympathetic to the American cause had either fled or were driven out. The city's population had plunged from 16,000 to around 6,000. With 3,000 reinforcements, the 7,000 redcoats actually outnumbered the remaining civilians. In those days, Boston was nearly an island, connected only by a narrow neck to the mainland, a situation that prevented either side from easily attacking the other, though minor skirmishes took place between detachments of American and British troops. The Americans destroyed a British war sloop that ran aground and disabled another with artillery fire. In late May Gage was joined by three generals—William Howe, Henry Clinton, and John Burgoyne—who would play decisive roles in the years ahead. Howe took command of the army, while Gage remained the provincial governor.

Howe was determined to break the stalemate and rout the rebels. Just a few hundred yards across Boston harbor was the headland of Charlestown, joined by a narrow neck to the mainland. Around fifteen hundred American troops commanded by William Prescott and Israel Putnam entrenched themselves atop two hills on that headland, with Bunker behind Breed's facing Boston. Rather than send his troops around the headland and land them at the neck, thus cutting off the rebel retreat, Howe decided on a direct assault of Breed's Hill. On the morning of June 17, the British fleet bombarded the American positions as twenty-two hundred redcoats were rowed across from Boston to Charlestown. The Americans repelled the first two assaults and most likely would have routed the third had they not run out of ammunition. They retreated to the mainland. The British cost of capturing the Charlestown headland was devastating—226 killed and 828 wounded, or nearly half those who marched up that hill, compared to around 450 American casualties; Prescott was among the dead.[5]

News of the victory at Bunker Hill and the redcoats' staggering losses further exhilarated Americans throughout the colonies and emboldened Congress to launch a series of initiatives that would bring the colonies ever closer to independence.

2

Congress, Strategy, and Secret Meetings

The Second Continental Congress had convened on May 10, 1775. The delegates spent weeks debating how to organize themselves, raise money, supply the army, and negotiate with the king and Parliament. Nonetheless, Congress made two key decisions that summer.

On June 15 Congress appointed George Washington the commander of the American army. Washington arrived in Boston four days later and set to work organizing, training, and feeding the army. Only when he had overcome those fundamental challenges could he embark on the even more daunting mission of driving the British from Boston.

The second decision was to bring Canada into the rebellion, ideally by diplomacy but if necessary by force. Delegate Samuel Chase expressed the pervasive belief that "the success of the war will, in a great measure, depend on securing Canada for our Confederation."[6] When Congress received no reply to its invitation to join the American cause, it approved a plan sent by Benedict Arnold to capture that province and appointed Gen. Philip Schuyler to command the expedition. When Schuyler appeared at Ticonderoga with his commission, Arnold angrily hurried off to Boston, where he talked Washington into granting him command of a separate expedition against Canada.

What transpired was a two-pronged invasion, with Schuyler and seventeen hundred men moving north down Lake Champlain toward Montreal, while Arnold and a thousand men headed up the Kennebec River, over the low divide, and down the Chaudière River to the St. Lawrence River just upstream of Quebec.

Gen. Richard Montgomery took command from Schuyler when he got sick. After a series of small battles, Montgomery took Montreal on November 13. Gen. Guy Carleton, the British commander of Canada, withdrew to Quebec. Meanwhile, Arnold's expedition did not begin until September. After a grueling 355-mile trek through the wilderness, they finally appeared before Quebec on November 14. Montgomery joined them on December 2. If the Americans could capture Quebec, they would control the St. Lawrence River Valley; cut off from supplies, the British posts on the Great Lakes would sooner or later capitulate. Congress would not learn that expedition's fate until early 1776.

For a majority in Congress, the siege of Boston and the campaign against Canada had one aim: reconciliation with Parliament on American terms. To that end, diplomacy paralleled the assertion of military power. On July 8 Congress dispatched to Whitehall what became known as the Olive Branch Petition. It included a plea to the king to intervene on their behalf with the cabinet and Parliament, along with an essay penned by Thomas Jefferson, titled "A Summary View of the Rights of British America."

The American diplomatic effort to seek reconciliation failed. By early October word reached Philadelphia that George III had sneeringly rejected the Olive Branch Petition. Instead, he had proclaimed on August 23 that the Americans were in rebellion, and, if they did not submit, all trade would be cut off on December 22, 1775.

That convinced a majority in Congress that they would have to seek foreign aid and possibly even allies. On November 29, 1775, Congress created the Committee of Secret Correspondence "for the sole purpose of corresponding with our friends in Great Britain, Ireland, and other parts of the world."[7] The first members of that nascent state department were Benjamin Franklin and John Dickinson of Pennsylvania, John Jay of New York, Thomas Johnson of Delaware, and Benjamin Harrison of Virginia.

The committee's first important act was to send instructions to Arthur Lee, the colonial agent for Massachusetts and New Jersey in London, to gather intelligence on British military plans and any Britons or foreigners who leaned toward the American cause. Within a week they learned firsthand of at least one sympathetic foreign government when an envoy was ushered into their presence.

Most French viewed the American rebellion as a godsend. They were still fuming over their humiliating defeat in the Seven Years' War, which had ended only a dozen years earlier. Under the 1763 Treaty of Paris, France surrendered its North American empire, along with many of its colonies in the Caribbean, West Africa, and India. Although most French longed for vengeance and the restoration of their political preeminence in Europe, they recognized that their country was not powerful enough to square off alone against Britain, and no other countries then had the interest, the power, or the will to join them. So Versailles simply had to bide its time.

The American rebellion offered at once a great opportunity and a danger for France. Clearly, the rebellion was devouring ever more British treasury, arms, and attention, which weakened the British elsewhere. American independence would be a devastating blow to the British Empire, but should France aid the rebels? What if Whitehall crushed the Americans, despite Versailles's efforts? Surely, Britain would then turn its guns against France. And with a navy only half the size and prowess of Britain's, France would most likely lose once again.

As the foreign minister, Charles Gravier, the comte de Vergennes, was King Louis XVI's chief adviser on the American rebellion. He needed more information about just how well led, armed, organized, and popular the rebellion was, so he initiated a secret diplomacy with the Americans. His envoy was Julien Alexandre Achard de Bonvouloir, a minor Foreign Ministry official. Bonvouloir reached Philadelphia in December 1775.

The timing of his arrival could not have been better. So far the Americans had inflicted bloody defeats on the redcoats in Massachusetts and Canada and besieged them in Boston and Quebec. Congress was coordinating efforts among the provisional colonial governments, raising troops, money, and supplies and conducting diplomacy. Ever more people enthusiastically embraced the American cause.

Bonvouloir was caught up in the heady atmosphere of Philadelphia. He reported, "Everyone here is a soldier. The troops are well clothed, well paid, and well commanded. They have about 50,000 volunteers who do not want pay."[8] He was wrong on every count. That delusion would be a godsend for the Americans and a disaster for the French, who would ground their policy in such exaggerated notions of American power, which would, in turn, swell actual American power.

The first of Bonvouloir's reports reached Versailles on February 27, 1776. Vergennes and his fellow ministers can be forgiven for believing in the vigor and the inevitability of the American cause. Vergennes then wrote up his own analysis of the implications of the rebellion for French interests and had his secretary, Joseph Mathias Gerard de Rayneval, do the same.

Their reports varied in emphasis but shared broad conclusions. The American revolt served French interests by weakening Britain; outright American independence would be a devastating blow to British power. This would thereafter render the British less aggressive as they calculated possibly antagonistic Americans in the international power balance. Those thirteen formerly closed markets would be open to French exports. In all, as Britain's relative power, wealth, and prestige diminished, that of France would rise. However, a reconciliation between Whitehall and the rebels could endanger France if they united against the remaining French colonies in the Caribbean. Thus, France should secretly send arms, munitions, and other war supplies to the rebels.[9]

Vergennes not only circulated his reports among the other ministers but began an effort to talk the Spanish into aiding the rebels. On March 1 he sent his thoughts to Geronimo de Grimaldi, his counterpart in Madrid. Although it would take longer for him to bring the Spanish on board, he forged a consensus for his proposed policy among the other ministers, with only Controller General Minister Anne Robert Jacques Turgot objecting that another war could bankrupt France. Then, armed with those reports and endorsements, Vergennes went to the king on May 2, 1776.

Louis XVI agreed to that bold shift in French policy and authorized a million livres for secretly buying and sending arms and munitions to the rebels. To obscure official French involvement, Vergennes created a front enterprise with a Spanish name, Rodrique Hortalez and Company, and named Pierre Augustin Caron de Beaumarchais to head it. The king then wrote to his Spanish cousin, Charles III, and asked him to join the effort. Charles III agreed to match that covert contribution to the rebels.

Beaumarchais was an excellent choice. Although he was then celebrated as the author of the *Barber of Seville* and other works of opera, prose, and poetry, he was an experienced intelligence operative, spoke English, was sympathetic to the American cause, and had gotten to know Arthur Lee in London. In late 1775 Beaumarchais sent Louis XVI and Vergennes his "Reflexions" and later his "Peace or War" essay to the king alone, in which he argued that it was in French interests to aid the rebels.[10]

During this time Congress was developing a diplomatic policy that complemented that of Paris. In response to Bonvouloir's mission, the secret committee of Congress decided to send America's first envoy overseas. On March 3, 1776, Silas Deane, a delegate from Connecticut, received the mission to journey to Paris with a wish list that included enough uniforms, muskets, and munitions for twenty-five thousand troops, along with a hundred cannons. Deane reached Paris on July 7 and soon was cordially received by Vergennes, who introduced him to Beaumarchais.[11]

Vergennes then sent Beaumarchais to London, where he secretly met with Arthur Lee and informed him of the front company that would funnel aid to the

Americans. Shortly after Beaumarchais returned to Paris, another agent from Vergennes appeared with the electrifying news that France would send the Americans 200,000 pounds sterling worth of arms and munitions via a Dutch vessel, which would probably transfer those supplies to an American ship at the Dutch colony of St. Eustatius in the Caribbean. On December 1, 1776, Congress received word from Lee of that vital shipment.

This shipment was independent of the supplies being transferred by Rodrique Hortalez and Company and initially underwritten by the 2 million livres contributed by Versailles and Madrid. The bill would soar. By October 10, 1776, an additional 3.6 million livres had been spent. Of the 5.6 million livres, 2.5 million livres had paid for clothing, 2.5 million livres for munitions and vessels, and 600,000 livres as wages for the officers and crews of those vessels. The first shipment alone included 30,000 muskets, 3,000 tents, 200 cannons, 27 mortars, 100,000 musket balls, and 13,000 cannonballs, which were packed into eight ships. This cargo was transferred to American vessels at Cap Francois, Saint Domingue.[12]

The diplomacy was in place. To be effective, however, the envoys needed to point to an American assertion of outright independence and the ability to defeat any British attempts to crush them. They would soon be able to claim one of those two essential requirements for open French and other foreign aid.

3

The Declaration of Independence

During the first half of 1776, the news from the war fronts was mixed. The American attempt to capture Quebec had failed miserably. Montgomery was killed and Arnold wounded leading assaults on the city during a snowstorm on the night of January 1, 1776. Yet that bad news was soon swept away by an astonishing feat. Washington drove the British army out of Boston on March 17. He did so by having most of the cannons that were captured at Fort Ticonderoga dragged by sledge through the snow to the Boston siege lines and emplaced on Dorchester Heights overlooking the British fleet. A deal was struck between Washington and Howe whereby if the Americans did not open fire, the British armada, packed with nine thousand troops and two thousand loyalists, would sail away to Halifax, Nova Scotia.

For the next several months there would be no British boots on the ground anywhere in the rebellious thirteen colonies. A British expedition led by Gen. Henry Clinton to take Charleston, South Carolina, and incite loyalists to rise against the rebels in the southern colonies had failed. In North Carolina a patriot force of militia routed a loyalist force at Moore's Creek Bridge on February 27. An American fort guarding Charleston repulsed an attempt by the British fleet to sail into the harbor on June 28. Clinton sailed away to join Howe in Halifax. John Murray, Lord Dunmore, the former governor of Virginia, led a small force of regulars, loyalists, and freed slaves, which captured Norfolk in June and sought to incite a slave rebellion against the rebels. But the Americans soon drove him and his small army away.

Perhaps no one person contributed more to America's eventual declaration of independence than Thomas Paine, an Englishman who sought his fortune in the colonies in November 1774 and soon became a fervent convert to the American cause. Although he joined the army, writing, rather than soldiering, was his true vocation. His "Common Sense" appeared in January 1776; within three months more than a hundred thousand copies had been sold.[13]

Paine's arguments were more emotional than intellectual, but he captured the feelings that countless Americans were unable or unwilling to articulate. He led with an attack on the king himself, something that few Americans, no matter how patriotic, had yet dared to do. His case was the intellectual equivalent of the little boy saying the emperor had no clothes. In doing so, he helped most of his readers sever the psychological fetters of mingled paternalism, affection, and fear that had bound them to George III and the British crown as a whole. That argument liberated none other than Washington himself; he and his officers stopped toasting the king at mealtime.[14] Paine then argued that the time had come for the colonies to declare independence.

Gradually, ever more members of Congress began openly to echo that call. Benjamin Franklin, on February 26, proposed that the colonies throw open their markets to all countries for two years, starting on July 20, 1776. A majority voted against that proposal, which they believed was synonymous with declaring independence. Then came word of Washington's bloodless victory at Boston. On April 6 Congress declared that America's markets were now open to all countries except Britain. Congress took a symbolic step toward independence on April 17, by renaming the Committee of Secret Correspondence the Committee for Foreign Affairs.

Although a consensus was building in Congress and beyond for outright independence, even the most fervent patriot leaders hesitated publicly to initiate such a dramatic and treasonous step. The assertion of national independence was spurred by word that Virginia, North Carolina, and New Jersey, along with ninety towns, had declared their own independence. The reticence in Congress ended on June 7 when Richard Henry Lee presented a resolution from the Virginia delegation that Congress "declare that these United Colonies are, and of right ought to be, free and independent states . . . and that all political connection between them and the state of Britain is, and ought to be, dissolved."

Congress approved the resolution and appointed a five-man committee, which included Benjamin Franklin, John Adams, Thomas Jefferson, Roger Sherman, and Robert Livingston, to draw up a formal declaration. Jefferson was appointed to draft the document, to be reviewed and, if necessary, altered by the other four.

Not only was Jefferson an accomplished stylist, but he was also an expert on classical and Enlightenment political philosophy, had penned "A Summary View of the Rights of British America" in 1774, and had helped George Mason draft Virginia's Bill of Rights.

The declaration is composed of two sections, with a summary of political liberalism followed by a list of American grievances against Britain's king and Parliament, justifying independence. The result is the most eloquent and succinct expression of political liberty rooted in natural law:

> We hold these truths to be self-evident, that all men are created equal; that they are endowed by their Creator with certain inalienable rights; that among these are life, liberty, and the pursuit of happiness; that to secure these rights governments are instituted among men, deriving their just powers from the consent of the governed; that whenever any form of government becomes destructive of these ends, it is the right of the people to alter to abolish it, and to institute a new government, laying its foundation on such principles, and organizing its powers in such form as to them shall seem most likely to effect their safety and happiness.

The committee approved Jefferson's draft with some minor changes on June 28 and then placed it before Congress. The delegates carefully scrutinized the document, line by line, and made their own corrections. Twelve of the thirteen delegations voted to approve the Declaration of Independence on July 2; John Hancock, the president of Congress, signed it on July 4. It did not become official until New York's delegation approved the document on July 19. Congress then printed and distributed copies of the Declaration of Independence throughout the new United States of America. Contrary to popular belief, it would take weeks after July 4 for representatives of all of the state delegations to sign the original document.

The declaration's intended audience was not only the American people and the British king and Parliament, but all of "mankind." It was designed not just to empower American diplomats to solicit recognition and support from other countries but to establish universal principles for political liberty, justice, government, and change. In the nearly two-and-a-half centuries since the declaration's words were first penned and published, countless peoples have acted on its principles. As such, perhaps few American acts have had a more powerful effect on humanity than the Declaration of Independence.[15]

4

From Brooklyn Heights to
the Delaware Crossing

George Washington paraded the army on July 9 and had the Declaration of Independence read to the soldiers. The site of that parade was New York City. After driving the British from Boston, he and his officers had pondered their next move. No one doubted that after replenishing his supplies and receiving reinforcements, Howe would be back. But where? New York was the obvious choice. If the British captured New York, they would sever the American coastline and be perfectly positioned to launch campaigns against New England and the mid-Atlantic colonies.[16]

During the spring Washington sent most of his army to New York and appointed a series of generals to the task of fortifying its approaches. By June he had 28,500 men on the muster rolls deployed in New York City and the surrounding islands and New Jersey. Desertion and sickness, however, gave him only 18,000 present and fit for duty.

Washington and his officers had correctly anticipated the British strategy. On June 29 the first vessels of the British armada sailed into New York bay and dropped anchor beyond cannon shot. By the time the last ships appeared on August 15, New York bay was crowded with 73 warships and 520 transports manned by 13,000 sailors and crammed with 32,000 troops, including 8,000 German mercenaries.

Gen. William Howe and his brother Adm. Richard Howe commanded, respectively, the invasion army and fleet, but they were empowered to make peace as well as war. They held royal commissions to issue pardons to all of those willing to lay down their arms and submit to the king's rule. The Howes understood that their ability to make peace depended on their success at war.

The first step was to disembark the army on Staten Island, chase off the handful of defenders, and secure the island as a base of operations. The second step was to land the army at the appropriately named Gravesend, on Long Island's southwestern tip, on August 22.

Two lines of American defenses lay north of the British army. The first was along a ridge stretching from the water's edge eastward across what is today central Brooklyn; about half the American army, or nine thousand men, was deployed along that ridge. The second was the crescent of redoubts and trenches on Brooklyn Heights just across from New York City at the southern tip of Manhattan Island.

The American defense along the ridge should have been formidable. Although a British victory was inevitable, given the army's overwhelming professionalism and numbers, it might have been bought with devastating Bunker Hill–type casualties. Unfortunately, Washington committed three elementary mistakes, which he would repeat numerous times in the years to come. First was his failure to establish a strict unity of command. He entrusted Brooklyn's defense first to Nathanael Greene, who got sick and was replaced by John Sullivan, who was then replaced by Israel Putnam. Each of those generals issued his own defense plans, which mostly sowed confusion among the regimental commanders. Second was Washington's failure to secure his flanks, or in this case, the eastern flank of his line along the ridge. Finally, he failed properly to reconnoiter the British Army.

Howe soon discovered the open American flank. On the night of August 27, he sent his elite division, commanded by Gen. Charles Cornwallis, around the back of the American army. When dawn broke, as Howe's other two divisions attacked the American front, Cornwallis led his men against the American rear. The American army suffered 970 dead and wounded, and 1,079 were taken prisoner; the British losses were light in comparison: 63 dead and 337 wounded. The rest of the Americans fled to the defenses on Brooklyn Heights.[17]

If not for a fortuitous combination of nature and resolve, Howe might have bagged Washington and half his army. With his Bunker Hill debacle in mind, Howe was naturally cautious in following up his victory with an immediate attack on the redoubts on Brooklyn Heights. Ideally, his brother could have sailed his warships between Manhattan and Brooklyn, cutting off Washington and bombarding the Americans into capitulation. But the wind was blowing steadily against that maneuver. And then, on the night of August 28, a thick fog blanketed New York Bay as Washington withdrew his entire army from Brooklyn to

Manhattan. Leaving a small force in New York City, Washington deployed most of the rest of his army in positions up Manhattan Island and beyond into the Bronx.

During the war, the Americans were aided by the leisurely, set-piece approach of eighteenth-century warfare. The campaign settled into a lull that lasted several weeks, as Howe consolidated his position in Brooklyn and sent out peace feelers. Meanwhile, Washington built up his own positions, massed supplies, and, most important, secured authorization from Congress to wage war without political oversight.

Eager to play for time, an American delegation, consisting of Benjamin Franklin, John Adams, and Edward Rutledge, asked to sit down with the Howe brothers. The two sides spoke cordially during a meeting on Staten Island on September 11. The Howes had very mixed feelings about the rebellion and the rebels. They genuinely liked Americans and sympathized with their grievances but were duty-bound, as military officers, to enforce the king's will. William Howe expressed his "gratitude and affection" for America "as for a brother, and if America should fall, he should feel and lament it like the loss of a brother." To that, with his keen humor, Franklin replied, "My Lord, we will do our utmost endeavors to save your lordship that mortification."[18] In the end the two sides talked past each other. The Americans were committed to independence, which the Howes were not authorized to discuss, let alone grant.

The next phase of the New York campaign opened on September 15 when Howe landed part of his army at Kip's Bay, about halfway up Manhattan's eastern shore. Once again the Americans were routed but managed to escape to the defenses on Harlem Heights with losses of only about seventy dead and two hundred prisoners. The following day the Americans retrieved a bit of self-respect when a detachment defeated an elite force of British light infantry and Highlanders that was scouting their lines, with each side suffering about a hundred casualties. That engagement rendered the normally cautious and methodical Howe ever more so. Then fire, most likely sparked by arson, broke out in New York on September 20, destroying about a quarter of the city and numerous supply warehouses before it was extinguished.

It was not until October 12 that Howe resumed the offensive. He landed a force at Throg's Neck, in what is today the southeast Bronx across from Long Island. He had hoped to march rapidly inland and turn the American flank but had not carefully reconnoitered that position. The "neck" is actually submerged at high tide, and American riflemen on the far shore picked off a number of redcoats, forcing Howe to withdraw the rest.

Howe's next move occurred on October 18, when he landed an even larger force at Pell's Point a half-dozen miles north. This time the British scattered the

Americans and established a strong foothold. Washington withdrew most of his army from Harlem Heights up to a clump of hills atop White Plains. He left behind about three thousand troops in Fort Washington, which faced Fort Lee across the Hudson River in New Jersey. His engineers told him that Fort Washington was impregnable, although those twin forts had not prevented British warships from sailing past up the Hudson River.

After massing his army, Howe launched an attack on Washington at White Plains on October 29. Once again, Washington let himself be outflanked, although his troops this time withdrew in good order to Castle Heights, five miles north. Once again Howe failed to vigorously pursue his defeated foe. After a careful reconnaissance, he decided that the American position would be too costly to assault, and so he encamped his army.

Leaving Gen. Charles Lee with seventy-five hundred troops at Castle Heights, Washington crossed the Hudson River at Peekskill with fifty-four hundred troops and marched down into New Jersey. He hoped that by splitting his army on either side of the Hudson River, while holding Fort Washington, he would compel Howe to divide his forces. That was a major miscalculation.

For now Howe ignored both Americans armies and concentrated on capturing Fort Washington in his rear. On November 2 he ordered his German mercenaries, known as Hessians because most of them came from Hesse, to assault the fort. When they overran the poorly constructed defenses, the fort's commander hastily surrendered his 3,000 men, along with tons of provisions and munitions and 161 cannons! It was a disastrous blow to the American cause, ranking only after the capitulation of a 5,000–man army at Charleston in 1780 as the worst defeat of the war.

This time Howe swiftly followed up his victory by landing six thousand troops under Cornwallis at the foot of the heights below Fort Lee on November 19. The redcoats scrambled to the top and into the fort, which Washington had ordered evacuated several days earlier. Unfortunately, the Americans had left behind large stores of munitions and provisions. Cornwallis then chased Washington across New Jersey until the Americans finally managed to put the Delaware River between themselves and their pursuers on December 8.

The American cause, confidence in Washington, and the army's strength were crumbling and by late December appeared ready to collapse completely. The enlistments of most of Washington's remaining troops were scheduled to expire on December 31. He could have simply waited until they headed for home and then gone into winter quarters with his remaining two thousand troops. Instead, he decided to launch a last blow against the British.

About 1,450 Hessians occupied Trenton just across the Delaware River. That was the last British encampment in a chain stretching across New Jersey to New Brunswick. Washington devised a brilliant and audacious plan. On Christmas night he would cross his army of twenty-four hundred troops and eighteen cannons at McKonkey's Ferry nine miles north of Trenton and then march south. Meanwhile, two other forces, Gen. John Cadwalader with eighteen hundred Pennsylvanian militia and Gen. Israel Putnam with a thousand troops, would cross the Delaware below Trenton and cut off the Hessian retreat in that direction.

It was a miserable night to be outdoors, let alone cross a river with a powerful current, march for miles and miles, and then fight a battle the next day. The temperature plunged, ice formed along the shores and pushed out toward midstream, and snow swirled and piled ever deeper. Cadwalader and Putnam decided to stay put in their encampments.

Washington stoically faced those miserable conditions and forged ahead. It took most of the night to cross the river with the few boats available. It was nearly dawn when he led his men toward Trenton. A mile from the town he split his army in two, sending John Sullivan's division directly against the town and Nathanael Greene's eastward to cut off any retreat and to block any British reinforcements from Princeton a dozen miles away.

The surprise was complete. The Americans fired volleys and then charged with leveled bayonets at the Hessians, who spilled from their quarters and tried to form into lines. The fighting did not last long. The Americans killed 22 and wounded 84 before 918 Hessians threw down their muskets and raised their arms in surrender. Unfortunately, 507 managed to escape south because Putnam and Cadwalader had failed to cross the river and block that route. Only a few Americans were wounded, and none died, except for two who had frozen to death during the night march. Washington withdrew across the Delaware on December 27 with his troops, the prisoners, and the captured supplies.[19]

That extraordinary victory may well have saved the American cause, as well as Washington's job. On December 28 Washington assembled his troops and offered them a ten-dollar bonus, nearly a year's pay, if they would stay another six weeks. At first not a man stepped forward. He appealed to their love of country and pride in themselves. Finally, a few men broke ranks and called out that they would fight on. Others joined them until nearly three thousand troops had rallied to their general's side.

Once again Washington had a bold plan. He led his army across the Delaware at Trenton on December 30, crossed Assunpink Creek south of town, and entrenched his men. His army swelled to five thousand men when generals Thomas

Mifflin and John Cadwalader marched up from Bordentown. Washington was confident that Cornwallis would march against him with his seven thousand troops at Princeton. But rather than remain at Trenton, Washington planned to circle behind Cornwallis and attack his rear at Princeton.

Washington posted riflemen several miles from Trenton on the road to Princeton. Those troops picked off dozens of redcoats and slowed Cornwallis's advance on January 1. It was late afternoon by the time Cornwallis reached Trenton. He ordered an attack across the creek, but the Americans repulsed it. Cornwallis then encamped his men and prepared for an all-out assault the next morning.

During the night, Washington left a few men behind to feed the campfires and make noise while he marched his army on a road that took him to Princeton by dawn. Once again he scored a complete surprise against the enemy. Cornwallis and his men were astonished to see the American camp empty in the early morning light. The British rear guard at Princeton was equally astonished to find the American army marching toward them. The Americans killed or wounded about 100 British and captured 230, along with the supply depot.

Washington then faced a tough choice. Should he continue to march eastward all the way to New Brunswick and capture that enormous supply magazine? If so, he could then turn on Cornwallis, who, shorn of provisions and munitions, might well surrender. But what if Cornwallis hounded him closely and then caught him between the garrison at New Brunswick? Then Washington would have to capitulate. Washington prudently chose to march north to the highlands around Morristown and there winter his tired but exultant army.

5

The Diplomatic Surge

Congress had no sooner declared independence than it got to work trying to solidify the new nation by seeking recognition, trade treaties, and alliances with the European states. A committee was assigned the task of drafting a model treaty of trade and amity to guide American diplomats and form the foundation for relations with other countries. The committee, which included Benjamin Franklin, John Adams, John Dickinson, Benjamin Harrison, and Robert Morris, submitted its model on July 18, but it was not until September 17 that Congress adopted the "Plan of 1776" with some modifications. The principles were free trade, free ships, free goods; the United States and its partners would reciprocally open their markets to one another, while during wartime, vessels from neutral countries could freely sail and carry goods to the ports of the belligerents. On September 24 Congress drafted instructions for diplomats over how best to negotiate the model treaty.[20]

The next step was to dispatch envoys to solicit official recognition, free trade, and, ideally, a military alliance. That diplomatic offensive would begin in Paris. The French had hinted that they might well transform their secret relationship into an open alliance if the Americans could score a decisive victory or two. If so, then other countries might follow suit. Meanwhile, the Americans could nurture unofficial relations with the other embassies in Paris.

Congress's first choice of envoys to join Silas Deane were Benjamin Franklin and Thomas Jefferson; Franklin accepted, Jefferson declined. The next choice was Arthur Lee, who was still in London. He replied that he would be happy to go.

Congress could not be accused of not thinking big. It instructed the delegation not only to fish for treaties of trade and alliance, but to try to either borrow or buy eight French ships of the line![21]

By the end of 1776, Benjamin Franklin, Arthur Lee, and Silas Deane had united in Paris. Deane had been in Paris since July 7, 1776, as a purchasing agent for Congress; Franklin arrived in Paris on December 21, 1776, and Lee the following day. On December 23 they wrote a letter to Vergennes requesting a meeting. Vergennes greeted them that day. They thanked him for the secret aid that France had provided and asked for more, along with recognition and an alliance.

Vergennes was friendly but noncommittal. For money, Vergennes sent them to the Farmers-General, a private group that collected taxes for the state and ran the tobacco monopoly. The Farmers-General agreed to give the Americans an advance on a tobacco shipment, even though getting it across the Atlantic past the British fleet and privateers would be a challenge.

Vergennes had the envoys introduced to Spanish minister Pedro Pablo Abarca de Bolea, the count of Aranda. The Americans expressed the same gratitude and made the same pitch to him. He explained that he was not empowered to negotiate with them, let alone officially recognize or ally with the United States. Such weighty decisions could only be addressed in Madrid.

Although the envoys were highly qualified, they made their share of mistakes as they tried to master the art of diplomacy. The worst was a carelessness when it came to security. Lee's secretary, John Thornton, was a British spy, as was one of Deane's secretaries, Edward Bancroft, and perhaps William Carmichael also. Although Franklin's grandson was his secretary, even he was not above suspicion. His father was William Franklin, the Tory New Jersey governor. Although the governor was estranged from both his father and his son, he might possibly have won back his son with a sincere attempt at reconciliation.[22]

The budding relationship between the Americans and the French was not free of tensions. Vergennes rebuked the delegation when American privateers tried to dispose of their prizes in French ports. He explained that to do so violated a French treaty with Britain as long as those nations were at peace. The prizes would have to be released.

As for relations with Spain, the envoys agreed that Arthur Lee should journey to Madrid and seek recognition, aid, trade, and alliance. To entice the Spanish, Congress was willing to help Madrid retake Pensacola. There was, however, a key catch. That aid depended on whether "the citizens and inhabitants of the United States shall have the free and uninterrupted navigation of the Mississippi and use of the harbour of Pensacola."[23] Learning of his mission, chief minister Pablo

Geronimo de Grimaldi met Lee at Vitoria to minimize any chance that the British would learn of the talks. To Lee's request and promise, Grimaldi made it clear that Spain was willing to provide some more secret aid but would not negotiate, recognize, or ally with the United States.

That policy was grounded in a careful analysis of Spanish interests. Charles III, Grimaldi, and most ministers not only spurned recognizing American independence, they hoped that rebellion against the monarchy would eventually fail, although only after gravely wounding British power. Madrid's ultimate nightmare was for the American rebels to inspire Spain's colonial subjects to demand reforms or outright independence. So the Spanish tried to walk that fine line between nurturing and restraining the rebels. To that end, Madrid issued secret orders to its port officials to let American privateers drop anchor and dispose of their prizes.

Versailles was far more generous. Beaumarchais organized nine ships packed with military supplies and dispatched them across the Atlantic in March 1777. Eight of those shipments would eventually evade the British blockade and reach American ports. Thanks to those supplies, the American armies fighting around Philadelphia and the upper Hudson Valley would be well supplied. By one estimate, 90 percent of the American army's weapons and munitions at Saratoga came from France. Without that, the surrender of Burgoyne and his army, and thus the war's turning point, most likely would have never taken place.[24]

6

Turning Points

Whitehall devised a strategy for 1777 that the ministers hoped would destroy the rebellion once and for all. Gen. John Burgoyne talked Lord George Germain, who was the acting war minister, into approving a plan to split the colonies in two. Three armies would converge at Albany and trap the enemy among them. Burgoyne himself would lead an eight thousand–man army down the Lake Champlain valley. Howe would advance up the Hudson River with half of his army, and a force of seven hundred British and hundreds of Indians under Lt. Col. Barry St. Leger would march from Lake Ontario. It was assumed that the Americans would mass their troops to block the passage of those armies. In doing so, they would be pushed back until they were cornered and crushed at Albany.

Like most plans, Burgoyne's made more sense at headquarters than it would in the field. One key problem was Germain's failure to consult Howe; instead, Germain merely informed him of his role. Howe would ignore Germain's vague order. Although, as the plan's author, Burgoyne knew exactly how his own campaign was supposed to unfold, actual execution would prove vastly more challenging. With naval superiority on Lake Champlain, getting to Fort Ticonderoga would be relatively easy. The difficulties would come in moving all his troops and supplies beyond that fort through the wilderness to the Hudson River. Finally, there was no guarantee that the Americans would be foolish enough to be trapped at Albany. Their best strategy was to fight delaying actions that ground down the redcoats, then sidestep the enemy's advance and harass its rear. They could then trap the British at Albany.

Howe's immediate objective was to bring Washington to battle. During the first half of 1777, British and American troops skirmished throughout New Jersey as each general tried to entice the other to fight on his own turf. Howe hoped to provoke Washington into marching his army down to the flatlands, where he would be overwhelmed by the superior numbers and the professionalism of the British and German troops. Washington was just as hopeful that Howe would attack his stronghold in the New Jersey highlands.

When it was clear that Washington would not play by his rules, Howe changed the game. By June he was determined to capture Philadelphia, America's largest city and capital. But that goal was self-defeating. The rebellion could only be crushed by destroying rebel armies, not seizing cities. Howe compounded that mistake. Inexplicably, he chose not to march his army the eighty miles from New York to Philadelphia, while sending the fleet around to secure a safe passage across the Delaware River. Instead, he packed most of his army aboard the fleet and waited for the winds to carry him to Philadelphia. He, his men, and his horses spent two miserable weeks crammed aboard those vessels before winds lifted the sails. It took another three weeks before the army had sailed down to Chesapeake Bay and then up it to Head of Elk. Most of the horses and the oxen died en route, and on August 23, when the men finally set foot on dry land, they were wobbly from inaction and disease.

Howe took nearly three more weeks before he felt that his army was ready to advance. Washington blocked his path east of Chad's Ford on the Brandywine River, twenty miles south of Philadelphia. Tragically, Washington failed to heed a crucial lesson from the previous year's humiliating New York campaign—once again he left a flank open. Howe quick-marched Cornwallis on a long detour that brought him behind Washington's right flank on September 11 and routed the Americans, inflicting nearly a thousand casualties while losing about six hundred men of his own.

Washington withdrew most of his army to Philadelphia but left Gen. Anthony Wayne and his brigade to hover at Paoli, west of the British advance. Howe launched a surprise bayonet attack on Wayne on the night of September 19, inflicted more than 150 casualties, and scattered the rest. This convinced Washington to abandon Philadelphia for a position about twenty miles north. Howe's army marched into Philadelphia on September 26 and then took up a defensive position a half-dozen miles north at Germantown. Congress, meanwhile, fled to York, Pennsylvania, sixty-five miles west.

While Howe's capture of Philadelphia appeared to be a terrible blow to the American cause, Benjamin Franklin cheerfully corrected the messenger who brought him the grim news: "No, Philadelphia has captured Howe!"[25] Franklin understood that rather than pursue Washington until he destroyed him, Howe would hole up in the comfort and safety of that city as he had in New York.

Once again Washington sought to retrieve the fortunes of the American cause and his own leadership by a bold attack—a double envelopment of the advanced British forces at Germantown, a half-dozen miles north of Philadelphia, on October 4. A thick fog hindered the Americans' advance. Nonetheless their initial attack forced the British to retreat. The Americans, however, made the mistake of besieging, rather than bypassing, a handful of redcoats holed up in a stone mansion called Chew House. That gave the rest of the British army crucial time to rally and counterattack. Washington ordered his army to retreat. Although Germantown was yet another American defeat, with losses of more than a thousand men, or twice the British casualties, the troops had nonetheless fought well.[26]

During late summer, the news from the New York frontier was ever more ominous. When Burgoyne's army moved south up Lake Champlain in late June, the opposing American army suffered some potentially crippling defects—it was poorly trained, equipped, and, above all, led. Congress had picked the generals for their prowess at politics rather than war. Generals Philip Schuyler and Horatio Gates had engaged in an unseemly and debilitating tug-of-war for command of the Northern Department. During the short term, Schuyler won the Pyrrhic victory. Crucial time was lost in bickering and backstabbing when the army needed to be reinforced, provisioned, trained, and entrenched.

Tragically, Congress had not even considered the best available general to command that front. Benedict Arnold had proved himself to be unsurpassed in daring, initiative, energy, and creativity as a tactician, a strategist, and a warrior who led from the front. He was renowned for his heroic exploits in the Fort Ticonderoga, Canada, and Basking Ridge campaigns. So far, his most decisive action was to build a fleet of gunboats on Lake Champlain and battle a British fleet to a bloody standstill at Valcour Island in autumn 1776. That delay prompted Gen. Guy Carleton to withdraw his army back to Canada, rather than try to capture Fort Ticonderoga. If merit was the criteria, Arnold should have commanded the New York front. But with ultimately disastrous results for the American cause, Congress snubbed him by continually appointing mediocrities with less abrasive personalities and much better political skills and connections. Arnold would eventually become so disillusioned that he would seek vengeance, power, and riches by betraying his country. Before that, however, he would lead the American army to two decisive victories against Burgoyne.

Yet another failure was putting timid Gen. Arthur St. Clair in charge of Fort Ticonderoga. He did nothing to retard Burgoyne's advance and then abandoned the fort and retreated on July 5 after the British appeared. Burgoyne sent his troops in hot pursuit. They caught up to the Americans and defeated them at Hubbardtown on July 7. Burgoyne then took a month to advance the twenty miles between Skenesboro at the southernmost navigable stretch of Lake Champlain and Fort Edward on the Hudson River. The rutted road was blocked with felled trees, which at times hid snipers. Once again, as Burgoyne's army approached, the Americans chose to flee, rather than fight, abandoning Fort Edward on July 28.

The American strategy of delay and retreat was actually sound. It made sense to trade territory for time and withdraw ever closer to the base at Albany, as Burgoyne's supply and communication lines stretched eventually to the snapping point. Burgoyne's army steadily weakened through battle and by the detachment of garrisons at strong points, while the American army swelled in numbers.

Meanwhile, St. Leger's campaign ground to a halt before Fort Schuyler, which guarded the divide between the Onondaga and Mohawk rivers. Col. Peter Gansevoort commanded the fort and rejected all demands to surrender. The crucial moment came on August 4, when the British and the Indians ambushed a relief expedition of eight hundred militia led by Gen. Nicolas Herkimer at Oriskany, a half-dozen miles away. Although St. Leger routed Herkimer, who lost more than four hundred men, along with his own life, Gansevoort ordered his troops to sortie, overrun the lightly defended British camp, and torch most of the supplies. The result was a standoff. St. Leger lacked the munitions and the heavy guns to destroy the fort, while Gansevoort lacked the men to drive him away.

Arnold led a second relief expedition and forced St. Leger to retreat without firing a shot. He sent ahead a simple-minded loyalist who excitedly informed St. Leger that the approaching American army was double its actual thousand troops. Most of the Indians grew discouraged and headed for home. St. Leger had no choice but to withdraw.

Despite Howe's victory at Germantown, his position was somewhat tenuous. Below Philadelphia, the Americans straddled the Delaware with Forts Mercer and Mifflin and a flotilla of gunboats. That prevented the British fleet from reaching Philadelphia. Supplies had to be carted by road from Head of Elk to the city through a hostile countryside filled with militia and sharpshooters.

Howe turned his attention to capturing those two forts. He first ordered an attack on Fort Mercer in New Jersey on October 22. The Americans routed the Hessians, inflicted four hundred casualties, and destroyed two British warships that sailed in to bombard the fort. This victory briefly raised American spirits.

The British then turned against Fort Mifflin; after suffering several days of bombardment, the Americans abandoned the fort on the night of November 16 and rowed across to Fort Mercer. As the British began a systematic siege, the Americans abandoned Fort Mercer on November 20.

Although they had lost those two forts, the Americans had helped divert Howe's attention from Washington, whose army was entrenched at Whitemarsh twenty miles north of Philadelphia. It was not until December 5 that Howe launched a probing attack. When the Americans repulsed that assault, Howe withdrew to his lines around Philadelphia. On December 19 Washington marched from Whitemarsh into winter encampment at Valley Forge, twenty-one miles west of Philadelphia. With the help of foreign instructors such as Friedrich Wilhelm Augustus von Steuben and Johann DeKalb, he spent those months drilling his men into professional soldiers.

Washington had more than just his army and the British to worry about. Faith in him among members of Congress and even in his own army had reached a low ebb. His supporters were able to defeat an attempt by a group known as the Conway cabal to replace him with Horatio Gates as commanding general.

In contrast to the defeats in Pennsylvania, the news from the New York frontier got steadily better and was finally triumphant. The Americans outright destroyed a largely German expedition detached by Burgoyne to capture the supply depot of Bennington, Vermont, and secure the eastern flank. A half-dozen miles west of Bennington on August 16, Gen. John Stark encircled and killed or captured more than eight hundred of the enemy while suffering only forty casualties. Henceforth, Burgoyne would have to continually look over his shoulder as he operated down the Hudson River.

Burgoyne's snail-paced campaign soon ground to a halt. Gates, who had wrested the command from Schuyler, entrenched his army on a plateau overlooking the Hudson about twenty-five miles north of Albany. Burgoyne ordered his army to attack on September 19. Although Gates wanted to sit tight in his entrenchments, Arnold disobeyed orders and led the army's left wing down against the British at Freeman's Farm and fought them to a bloody standstill; the Americans suffered 321 casualties while inflicting nearly twice as many on the British.[27]

Arnold's decisive action stirred Gates with jealousy rather than gratitude. He removed Arnold from field command. Arnold would sulk Achilles-like in his tent until Burgoyne launched his next attack.

That attack would not come for another three weeks. The ferocity of Arnold's assault and the high casualties the British suffered had spooked Burgoyne into entrenching his own army. He and most of his officers were thoroughly discouraged.

His troops and supplies had dwindled steadily during nearly four months of campaigning through the wilderness. He had suffered crucial defeats at Bennington and Freeman's Farm. The American position on the heights blocking the road to Albany seemed impregnable. Even in the unlikely event that he could drive the enemy from those heights, the cost in casualties could be crippling, and he would still face further battles on the long road south to Albany.

So Burgoyne and his generals decided to sit tight and await rescue. They knew that in the previous month, Gansevoort's stalwart defense of Fort Schuyler and Arnold's advance had forced St. Leger to withdraw. So they pinned their hopes on an advance from Howe up the Hudson. Howe, of course, was in Philadelphia. A British expedition led by Gen. Henry Clinton did sail up the Hudson, capture the forts and rout the troops guarding the highlands, burn Kingston, and get as far as Livingston Manor forty miles south of Albany before turning back.

Somehow a messenger with word of Clinton's withdrawal slipped through the American lines and into Burgoyne's camp. That devastating news, combined with reports of American raids on his supply lines, provoked a near panic among Burgoyne and his officers. Rather than immediately retreat, they agreed to try to outflank the American lines. Early on the morning of October 7, Burgoyne sent his right wing forward.

Once again, Arnold mounted his horse and led an American attack on the British as they marched across Freeman's Farm. The Americans drove the redcoats back into their entrenchments, killing and wounding more than 600 and capturing more than 200, while suffering only about 140 casualties. Arnold was among the wounded, having been struck with a musket ball in the same leg that was wounded at Quebec. Once again, Gates was enraged at Arnold's decisive and courageous leadership.

Burgoyne retreated slowly back up the Hudson. Gates managed to cut off his retreat at Saratoga. The Americans outgunned the British by 13,000 to 5,763, with only 3,400 fit for duty. Burgoyne asked for terms. Gates foolishly did not demand unconditional surrender but instead accepted Burgoyne's request that his army be paroled and returned to Britain. The two signed a convention on October 17. Fortunately, Congress rejected that agreement and ordered the British army interned for the duration.

7

The Alliance with France

B urgoyne's surrender was the war's turning point. The British had not only
failed in their attempt to split the colonies in two but lost an entire army
in the gamble. American morale soared as British morale plummeted. Most
important, Saratoga encouraged the French finally to take the plunge and ally
openly with the United States.

The heartbreaking news of Burgoyne's surrender at Saratoga reached London on
December 3. Whitehall reacted with uncharacteristic speed. The following day it dispatched Paul Wentworth, a former lobbyist agent for New Hampshire, to Paris to meet
with the Americans and find out just what it would take to reconcile the relationship.
Wentworth and Deane met on December 15 and 16 and then together with Franklin
on January 6, 1778. Although Wentworth was not empowered to negotiate, he was allowed to offer each American a high post and a salary in the British government if the
rebels laid down their arms and rejoined the empire. Yet the Americans stuck to their
mission. They repeatedly explained that the United States desired from Britain nothing less than the recognition of its independence. The Wentworth mission died.

The French were exuberant when they learned on December 7 of Burgoyne's
fate. The result would be a complete transformation of the political calculus at
Versailles. That policy shift was spurred when Vergennes heard of Wentworth's
mission. Would the British offer the Americans an irresistible package of concessions? Franklin eagerly played on that French fear, warning Vergennes that he
could nip any budding rapprochement with "the immediate conclusion of a treaty
of commerce and alliance."[28]

41

Vergennes believed that he had to take a decisive step. On December 17 he informed Franklin that he would convince the king and his council to agree to treaties of both alliance and commerce with the United States. It took him only a couple of weeks to do so, despite the disappointing reality that Spain would not for now join the alliance against Britain. On January 8, 1778, Vergennes informed the Americans that the king had approved his proposal. All that remained was to work out the details of the two treaties.[29]

Benjamin Franklin, Silas Deane, and Arthur Lee signed with Joseph Mathias Gerard de Rayneval, Vergenne's deputy, two treaties on February 6, 1778, one of alliance and the other of trade. The Treaty of Amity and Commerce was nearly identical to the model treaty composed by Congress—the ports of each country would be freely open to the other on the basis of the most favored nation principle. The Treaty of Alliance bound the United States and France to five major commitments to each other. They would war as allies until the United States won its independence. They would accept other states in their alliance, with a side agreement pointedly reserving a place for Spain. They would negotiate a mutually acceptable peace with Britain. Afterward, their relationship would continue indefinitely as a defensive alliance whereby each would aid the other if it were the victim of aggression. Finally, the United States pledged to guarantee French possessions in the New World "forever."[30]

Although each of the tenets seemed like a good idea at the time, most would be troublesome in the coming years. The worst was the open-ended defensive alliance between the United States and France. Another was the promise of no separate peace. The idea of treaties of alliance and trade between an absolute monarchy and a republic in rebellion against a constitutional monarchy was not so much a real problem as it was an ideological paradox. Yet another issue was the status of "the United States." In listing all thirteen states as the United States, sovereignty appeared to lay in them.

Finally, there was no mention of just what territory constituted the United States. The Americans and the French alike were committed to American independence more as an idea than as a place. Congress itself would not address that vital question for several years. Even after doing so, only war and diplomacy could ultimately determine the outline of the new nation. While ever more Americans wanted their country to extend westward to the Mississippi River, the French and the Spanish hoped to straitjacket the United States between the Atlantic Ocean and the Appalachian Mountains.

Silas Deane would bear the treaties back to Congress. Franklin and Lee must have watched him go with very mixed feelings. Relations among the three had never been good. Clashes of ego, ambition, and outlook caused Deane and Lee to despise each other, while Franklin had his doubts about them both. Lee accused Deane of using public funds for private financial speculations. The charges were true, and Lee sent back to Congress the evidence to prove them. In November 1777 a majority in Congress agreed to recall Deane. Although he would receive his recall, he returned with the hope that the treaties he laid before them would inspire them to dismiss the accusations against him. That hope was misplaced.

With the British occupying Philadelphia, Congress was at York. Deane's arrival with the treaties on April 30 stirred a celebration. New York delegate Henry Livingston captured the prevailing elation that "America is saved by almost a miracle."[31] Congress unanimously ratified both treaties on May 4, 1778.

Meanwhile, Vergennes succeeded in maneuvering the British into first declaring war. Rumors of the two treaties seeped through Paris and London. On March 13 France's minister to Britain verified one of those rumors by informing the North cabinet of the commercial treaty between France and the United States. Yet he was instructed to delay confirming the alliance as long as possible while Versailles completed its war preparations. Britain declared war on France on March 17, 1778. King Louis XVI followed suit with his own war declaration and officially recognized the American commissioners at Versailles on March 20, 1778. The first blood flowed on June 17, when British warships attacked a lone French frigate in the English Channel.

Ever since Vergennes had talked Louis into secretly supporting the American rebellions, he also secretly had the army and navy ministers prepare their respective forces. Those efforts had accelerated as the policy shifted from covert aid into an overt alliance and war with Britain.[32]

The increase in warships ready for action was especially impressive. The number of French ships of the line soared from 37 in January 1777 to 52 in July 1778. Although the British had 66 ships of the line at sea that summer, and their navy outnumbered the French fleet by 122 to 63 warships of all sizes, Versailles hoped to make up that two-to-one disadvantage in three ways. First, Versailles launched a major warship-building effort. During the war, French shipyards would christen twenty-nine ships of the line, which would more than make for the nineteen lost in combat. Second, Versailles hoped soon to entice Spain into an alliance against Britain; the combined fleets would equal that of Britain, at least in numbers. Finally, Britain's warships were scattered in flotillas in the English Channel, along the American seaboard, and in the Caribbean, with smaller contingents in the Mediterranean and the Indian Ocean. The French would have the advantage of concentrating their forces at crucial points and overwhelming the British. And that advantage would be magnified if Spain could be enticed into the alliance.[33]

In contrast, Britain was ill-prepared for war with France and hoped to end the war with the Americans before its forces were seriously engaged. The cabinet hastily appointed and dispatched envoys to Philadelphia, where they would join with William and Richard Howe in convincing the Americans to lay down their arms. The commissioners included Frederick Howard (5th Earl of Carlisle), William Eden, George Johnstone, and Adam Ferguson. The Carlisle Commission was empowered to offer amnesty for all, repeal of internal taxes, recognition of Congress as a legitimate body subject to Parliament's supremacy, and the army's withdrawal—in other words, the Americans were essentially being offered home rule. The envoys, however, were not empowered to negotiate but were merely to present those terms for the Americans to take or leave. Carlisle also carried orders for Howe to abandon Philadelphia and turn over his command to Gen. Henry Clinton.

Congress actually learned of the Carlisle Commission ten days before Deane arrived with his treaties. Even then, the British offer was too little, too late. As Gen. John Sullivan put it, "had proposals of this kind been properly & sincerely made by the Court of Britain to the Supreme Authority of America, before the wanton cruelty which has marked the progress of British arms in this country had taken place, or prior to our declaring ourselves independent and entering into an alliance with foreign powers, they would have been accepted with sentiments of gratitude."[34]

Instead, the Americans saw the Carlisle Commission as a sign of weakness. George Washington expressed the prevailing view when he described Whitehall's diplomatic ploy as "a compound of fear, art, villainy, and these ingredients are so equally mixed, that I scarcely know which predominates."[35] The Americans stood firm on independence and barred those British envoys from crossing the lines.

8

The Widening War

Militarily, the mere announcement that France had allied with the United States led to an American victory. Fearing that a French armada would bottle up the British army in Philadelphia by sailing into Delaware Bay, Whitehall ordered Gen. Henry Clinton to withdraw to New York. Clinton began evacuating Philadelphia and crossing his army to New Jersey on June 18. That potentially hazardous operation took days.

Washington did not take advantage of that opportunity to strike but instead crossed the Delaware north of Philadelphia and shadowed the slow British march across New Jersey. He was right to be cautious. The British army numbered about 20,000 troops to his own 11,800.

The Americans caught up to the British rear guard near Monmouth, New Jersey, on June 28. Washington ordered an all-out assault. Once again, a subordinate failed to properly execute his plan. Gen. Charles Lee was the field commander. When the British stood firm, repulsed his initial attack, and then advanced, Lee panicked and ordered a retreat. Washington galloped up, rallied his army, dismissed Lee with a tongue-lashing, and ordered a counterattack.

The battle of Monmouth was both a tactical and a strategic draw. Each side lost about three hundred men and held most of its ground. Strategically, Clinton did not turn his army around and launch it against Washington but instead hurried his men on to the safety of New York. Nor did Washington hotly pursue Clinton and force him to turn and fight again. Yet emotionally it was an important American victory. Months of drilling at Valley Forge had empowered the Americans to fight the redcoats to a standstill and prove that their professionalism was as great as their courage and convictions.

Washington deployed his army in an arc from New Jersey to the Hudson Highlands to Connecticut to block any British advance from New York City. He dispatched Gen. John Sullivan to Rhode Island to retake Newport from the British. Sullivan soon had some hefty reinforcements.

Not long after signing the two treaties with the United States, Versailles acted. Adm. Charles Hector, comte d'Estaing's fleet of twelve ships of the line, four frigates, and several scores of transports packed with supplies and four thousand troops, dropped anchor off the mouth of New York Bay on July 7, 1778. Unfortunately, the fleet was too heavily laden to cross the shallow waters at the bay's mouth. D'Estaing sent word to Washington of his arrival and asked for instructions. Washington asked d'Estaing to sail to Newport and help Sullivan recapture that strategic port, which the British had held since December 6, 1776.

The combined operation opened on August 9 when d'Estaing's fleet sailed into Narragansett Bay and Sullivan's army marched to meet them at Howland's Ferry. The plan was for the American and French troops to land on Newport Island and then march against the British fortifications guarding the port. That plan died abruptly when word arrived that a British fleet of thirteen ships of the line and two frigates under Adm. Richard Howe had appeared at the mouth of Narragansett Bay. D'Estaing sailed forth with his fleet and engaged Howe. As each fleet maneuvered to gain the wind advantage, a hurricane blew in and battered both for three hellish days and nights. When the storm finally abated, both fleets were scattered and damaged. D'Estaing retired to Boston to refit his fleet.

That decision soured the relationship. Sullivan rather unfairly blasted the French for abandoning the siege. Sullivan had crossed over his army to Newport Island but without French support had to withdraw before a British advance. The French fleet anchored in Boston from August 29 until late December, when d'Estaing ordered anchors weighed for the West Indies. During that time, the alliance hardly prospered. Americans and French sailors engaged in several tavern and street brawls over provisions, alcohol, women, and a century and a half of rage over their past wars to dominate North America's eastern third. In all, the Franco-American alliance could not have had a more inauspicious start.

The New York City front was also stalemated. Washington was not strong enough to attack Clinton, and Clinton lacked the resolve to sally forth with most of his army and try to run down and destroy Washington. Clinton's excuse was that after France joined the war, he had to dispatch more than eight thousand of his troops to reinforce Newport, Florida, and British colonies in the West Indies. He did send out large forces to raid the countryside and probe American defenses. Because Washington's divisions were so widely scattered, they could not concentrate swiftly enough to crush any of those British expeditions. The result was plenty of skirmishes but no decisive battles.

Ever more of the war was fought along the American frontier.[36] Since the war's outbreak, Congress had struggled and failed to keep peace with the Indians. The frontier was divided into eleven regions, with an Indian commissioner appointed to each. That diplomacy failed with most tribes for several reasons. First of all, Congress lacked the money to buy the gifts that might have helped keep the peace. More important, Congress lacked the authority to prevent pioneers from settling lands claimed by the Indians. In contrast, the British did have the wealth to pile gifts on the Indians in council, while traders, rather than settlers, passed through Indian lands.

From 1776 onward, Indians began raiding the New York, Pennsylvania, Kentucky, Tennessee, North Carolina, South Carolina, and Georgia frontiers, and with each year those raids grew more destructive and killed or displaced more settlers. The war's most devastating attack came in June 1778 when a British and Indian force attacked the Wyoming Valley in the Susquehanna Valley, killed more than four hundred settlers, destroyed eight forts, burned nearly all of the buildings in the region, and sent hundreds of survivors fleeing to safety.

The Americans did score some important, if not decisive, victories on the frontier. In Kentucky Daniel Boone is the best known of a half-dozen leaders who were able to rally dwindling numbers of settlers to stay and fight off repeated attacks. On the Carolina frontier, yearly expeditions were launched against the Cherokees. Yet the most dramatic campaigns were led by George Rogers Clark, a Virginian frontiersman who was among Kentucky's first settlers.

Clark was determined to carry the war against the British forts that gave supplies, arms, and advisers to the Indian raiders. In April 1778 he received a colonel's commission and funds from Governor Patrick Henry and the Virginia assembly to raise and lead an expedition against the British forts in the upper Mississippi River Valley. In July, with a couple of hundred men, Clark seized Kaskaskia and Cahokia on the Mississippi River and sent a force to capture Vincennes on the Wabash River. With barely a shot fired, Clark had shifted the military and thus diplomatic balance toward America in that frontier region. In far-away Paris, American negotiators would eventually use that and other western operations to assert a claim for a United States that extended to the Mississippi River.

The British were determined to restore control over that corner of the frontier. Lt. Col. Henry Hamilton, Detroit's commander (known as the "Hair-Buyer," for purchasing American captives and scalps from the Indians), led an expedition that retook Vincennes in December 1778. From there, he intended to set forth in the spring to recapture Kaskaskia and Cahokia.

Learning of that loss, Clark was not content to sit tight and await Hamilton. Instead, he gathered his men and led them on a grueling 150-mile march through the wilderness and the flooded lowlands from Kaskaskia to Vincennes in February 1779. Through diplomacy, Clark was able to convince most of the local Indians to abandon their support of Hamilton. Then he and his men captured a returning expedition that had raided Kentucky and brought back scalps. Clark had five of the raiders lined up facing the fort and ordered them put to death; wielding a tomahawk, the executioner bashed in the skull of each. Clark warned Hamilton that if he did not immediately surrender unconditionally, he and his men would suffer the same fate. Hamilton prudently handed over his sword.

That victory did not end warfare in the Ohio valley. British and Indians continued to launch raids against the Kentucky settlements. Increasingly, though, the frontiersmen struck back with expeditions from Kentucky and Pittsburgh against Indian villages in what is now Ohio. The largest battle on that front was a British and Indian victory in 1782 at Blue Licks, where they killed and wounded more than a hundred Kentuckians.

The war's largest expedition, however, was launched against the hostile Iroquois of western New York state in 1779. Washington assigned Gen. John Sullivan the mission of massing more than five thousand troops and destroying the Seneca, Onondaga, and Cayuga tribes. His campaign did not kill many Indians, but he did succeed in burning nearly all of the Iroquois villages whose inhabitants fled to safety, as well as supplies at Fort Niagara on Lake Ontario. Although he had plenty of troops and supplies, Sullivan failed to push on and attack Fort Niagara. Had he done so, he would have undoubtedly taken that undermanned fort and thus cut off all of the British posts in the upper Great Lakes, decisively shifting military and diplomatic power in the Northwest.

To win independence, it was essential for the Americans to defeat the British on as many fronts as possible. The reality that Britain was the world's greatest naval power failed to deter the Americans from warring at sea. Congress founded the American navy in 1775 and began constructing what would eventually amount to thirteen frigates. That effort took considerable time and money. In the end, none of those warships ever captured a single British ship. Instead, the British managed to capture the only American ship that actually made it to sea and destroyed or blockaded the others.

Yet the Americans did prove their mettle at naval warfare in another way. Congress and the states issued seventeen hundred letters of marque to enterprising sea captains, authorizing them to convert their vessels into warships and sail forth against British shipping. Hundreds of British vessels were captured and sold with their cargoes in the United States or in foreign ports. British attacks on American shipping, however, were just as rapacious.[37]

Actual naval battles between American and British warships were rare. The war's most ambitious American naval action was an attack of eight small sloops and schooners led by Cdre. Ezek Hopkins against New Province in the Bahamas in 1776. They overran the town and brought its vast stores of naval supplies, munitions, and cannons, along with a half-dozen vessels, back to Philadelphia. Capt. John Barry was the first American to capture a British warship, the sloop *Edward* in 1776. The most intrepid captain was John Paul Jones, who captured scores of merchant ships during the war. His most famous battle was against the fifty-four-gun HMS *Serapis*, which he captured with his own ship, the twenty-eight-gun *Bonhomme Richard*, which sank beneath him and his crew in September 1779.

9

Foreign Intrigues

Americans celebrated Conrad Alexandre Gerard's arrival at Philadelphia on July 12, 1778. Congress and the public alike initially treated him with all the gratitude, respect, and deference that they believed was due the first foreign diplomat accredited to the United States. Congress reciprocated by appointing Benjamin Franklin as America's first minister to France; he would receive his promotion a few months later.

Gerard would pass more than two years in the United States until ill health and perhaps emotional exhaustion forced him to return to France in October 1779. During that time, he seems never to have felt any warmth for the American people or sympathy for their cause. Aloof and at times imperious, he disdained democracy as chaotic, boisterous, and ill-mannered. Nonetheless, of the two key goals that Vergennes assigned him, Gerard amply fulfilled one and made considerable progress on the other.[38]

Gerard succeeded in diminishing a century and a half of American fear and hatred toward the French, whom the Americans associated with popery, frontier war, Indian raids, and atrocities. Although that threat had disappeared when the 1763 Treaty of Paris had split France's North American empire like a wishbone between the British and Spanish empires, the animosity and distrust lingered. Gerard repeatedly assured all those concerned that France had no designs on reconquering its former North American empire of Canada and Louisiana but simply wanted to restore its fishing rights off the Newfoundland Banks and bolster the security of its Caribbean sugar islands by eroding British power.[39]

The other part of Gerard's mission, however, made him ever more the center of controversy. Vergennes envisioned a United States squeezed between the Appalachian Mountains and the Atlantic Ocean, big enough to be a perpetual thorn in the side of Britain but contained far from Spain's New World empire and even farther from France's Caribbean colonies. To that end, Gerard was to do all he could to undermine any American attempts to take Canada, the Floridas, and land west of the Appalachians and to gain navigation rights on the Mississippi River or access to the Newfoundland fisheries. As such, he was promoting Spanish as much as French interests, even before those countries had formally aligned.

To make that unpopular case, he had to hold his nose and plunge into the maze of American politics, going so far as to shamelessly pay off politicians and editors. He provoked the most controversy for championing Silas Deane against charges of financial impropriety in Paris. That scandal did not end after Deane returned bearing the treaties with France; it worsened. Deane became a symbol for those who were worried that the alliance with France entangled America in European venality and corruption. What happened to Deane in Paris could happen to any hapless or willing Americans who dealt with French officials not only abroad but even at home. Gerard exacerbated those fears and resentments by overplaying his hand. He went so far as to try to get Congress to recall Arthur Lee; however, a majority in Congress refused to do so.

Gerard's machinations aided the United States in at least one way. He forced Congress sooner, rather than later, to debate just what kind of peace it wanted. While support for independence was rock solid in Congress, everything else was up for grabs. The result was a chronic, multistranded tug-of-war among lobby groups. Each industry—fishing, farming, shipbuilding, commerce, finance, and manufacturing—had its own specific agenda. And then there were regional differences. New Englanders and, to a lesser extent, New Yorkers favored retaining their privileges in the Newfoundland fisheries and trade with Britain and its other colonies while, ideally, taking part or all of Canada. The middle and southern states wanted to expand to the Mississippi River Valley and the Gulf Coast and were much less interested in foreign trade.

It took nearly eight months of debate in 1779 before Congress determined just what peace terms would be acceptable. A committee wrote up a secret list on February 23. Number one on the list was that negotiations could only follow British recognition of American independence. As for territory, the United States would, at a minimum, include all land west to the Mississippi River, south to the 31st parallel latitude, and north beyond the Great Lakes to include all of Ontario along 45 degrees latitude through Lake Nipissing to the headwaters of the St.

Croix River and down it to the Atlantic Ocean. The United States would retain fishing rights and drying rights on the seas and the shores of eastern Canada, especially on the Newfoundland Banks. Americans would have the right to navigate the Mississippi River to the sea.[40]

This position essentially gave something to every major interest group. With near universal satisfaction, Congress approved a final version of the instructions on March 24. Although numerous resolutions were submitted by various parties to alter parts of the instructions, that peace policy would remain essentially unchanged for two years before it was radically redrawn.

All along, Gerard did everything possible to throw cold water on American ambitions. His spies kept him well informed of the debates within secret sessions of Congress and its committees. He knew the essence of the report at least a week before it was released and tried to snuff any hopes for it beforehand. In a speech before Congress on February 15, 1779, Gerard warned that Madrid would oppose any claims of territory or rights on territory it considered its own: "Spain wished to see the territorial claims of the United States terminated. She wishes to have the navigation of the Mississippi shut, and possession of the Floridas."[41]

Although that message was profoundly discouraging, most Americans reasoned that even if Spain was recalcitrant, surely their ally Louis XVI would champion their ambitions. Gerard disabused them of that notion on May 22, 1779. France was solely committed to American independence—the exact details of any peace treaty would depend on the prevailing distribution of power among those states at war and their respective diplomats.[42]

Nonetheless, Congress stood firm. Recognition of that frontier and navigation rights on the Mississippi River were not all that the Americans wanted from Spain. For George Washington, the alliance with France was certainly essential to keeping the Americans in the fight, but he worried that even a French fleet and army would not be enough to defeat the British. He argued that an alliance with Spain should swiftly follow one with France. To Congress he explained that "if the Spaniards would but join their fleets to France and commence hostilities, my doubts would all subside. Without it I fear the British navy has it too much in its power to counteract the schemes of France."[43]

Congress had already made and failed in one attempt to open relations with Spain. After Grimaldi politely showed Arthur Lee the door at Vitoria in 1776, few in Congress harbored any illusions that forging relations with Madrid would be an easy task. Yet they viewed an alliance with that absolute monarchy as crucial to winning American liberty. They reckoned that there was little to lose and potentially much to gain by another attempt.

The Spanish had a very clear-headed understanding of just how the American rebellion related to their national interests. Charles III had been willing to match his cousin's contribution of a million livres to Rodrique Hortalez and Company in 1775. But since then, he had resisted requests that Spain join with France in warring against Britain. His foreign ministers—Grimaldi until 1777 and Jose Monino y Redondo, count de Floridablanca since then—had supported the policy of at once aiding the American rebels while opposing their independence.

Although Madrid had no intention of recognizing the United States, it did dispatch Don Juan de Miralles to Philadelphia to gather intelligence. Miralles reached Boston on January 8, 1778, and would eventually spend time with Congress and Washington's army. When he died of illness in Morristown, he would be replaced by Francisco Rendon. Madrid would also continue to give financial aid to the Americans, mostly through a front company known as Don Diego Cardoqui and Sons of Bilbao.

A year after France declared war on Britain, Charles and Floridablanca decided that it was in Spain's interests to ally openly with his cousin. Like Louis, Charles hoped to provoke a British war declaration. First, he offered to mediate peace between the Americans and the British. Neither side took his offer seriously. The Americans wanted him not as a mediator but as an ally; they ignored the unofficial word from Spanish officials that Madrid would not recognize American independence. The British feared that the Spanish would follow the French lead and favor the Americans. Floridablanca then issued on April 3, 1779, an ultimatum to Britain's minister in Madrid, Lord Grantham, that Gibraltar was the price for Spain's continued neutrality. But he did not wait for an answer.

The Bourbon "Family Compact" referred to the cousins who sat atop the thrones of France and Spain. More often than not, one would ally with the other when it went to war. The latest version was made official on April 12, 1779, with the Convention of Aranjuez allying Spain and France. A grand secret deal was cut whereby Spain would regain Gibraltar, Minorca, and the Floridas, while France retook the Newfoundland fisheries, Senegal, and Dominica in the Caribbean; they would keep fighting until Spain retook Gibraltar, at the very least.

Charles III issued a war declaration against Britain on June 21, 1779. Yet Spain had no sooner gone to war than Madrid extended secret feelers to London for a way out. What the king and his ministers wanted was to intimidate the British into concessions without a decisive clash of arms. So the Spanish played parallel and at times overlapping games of war and diplomacy. That strategy eventually failed. The Spanish would have to take what they wanted. To the surprise of many, they would be quite successful in doing so, at least for a while.

The alliance between France and Spain against Britain was certainly in American interests. The thinner Britain's troops, sailors, and cash were spread, the greater the chance for an American victory. Yet a potentially grave problem lurked in that alliance. Because America's alliance with France bound them both to no separate peace, that meant that the United States now would have to continue warring against Britain until Spain took Gibraltar or gave in. Not only did the Spanish continue to refuse to recognize, let alone ally with, the United States; they were apparently willing to use the war to take territory such as the Floridas that many Americans eyed for their own country. Thus was America's fate entangled with that of far more powerful states with often diametrically opposed interests.

That was not the only drawback. Well before Spain entered the war, Vergennes had been trying to get the Americans to accept Spain's territorial claims in the Floridas and between the Mississippi River and the Appalachian Mountains. He would seek to convince Congress to grant him the authority to supervise any American negotiations with the British in Paris.

Although relations with Spain were crucial to America's independence struggle, Congress did not get around to appointing an envoy to Madrid until early autumn 1779. That institution was overburdened with trying to finance the war and forging a consensus among the states on countless other issues, both essential and trivial. On September 27 Congress issued John Jay official instructions to get the Spanish government to accept the free navigation of the Mississippi River to the sea; a trade treaty; a boundary at the 31st degree latitude; ideally, a grant of $5 million, but, if necessary, a loan of not more than 6 percent interest; and an alliance. As if that wish list were not daunting enough, Jay made quite a sacrifice in accepting the mission—he had to resign as both the president of Congress and chief justice of New York's supreme court![44]

And then there was the challenge of getting from Philadelphia to Madrid. A series of trials along the way—storms, damaged ships, prowling British warships, and Spanish red tape—prevented Jay from reaching Madrid until April 4, 1780. He would remain there for more than two frustrating years, as Spanish officials rarely spoke to him, let alone recognized his status. He did meet frequently with France's minister to Spain, Armand Marc, the comte de Montmorin de Saint-Herem, but Montmorin proved to be a false ally and worked with Floridablanca to undercut Jay's diplomacy.

Floridablanca had John Jay, along with his secretary William Carmichael, ushered before him for their first meeting on May 11. Thereafter, the Spanish minister would condescend to meet Jay only a handful of times, although they did exchange many letters. His policy was to keep the American rebellion alive barely enough to drain British power, but not enough to triumph. To that end, Floridablanca in Madrid and Governor Bernardo de Galvez in New Orleans would periodically rummage in the king's coffers for a series of small loans that eventually amounted to $174,011 and $74,087, respectively, to the American envoys John Jay and Oliver Pollack. Those bank drafts were written in ways that precluded Spanish recognition of American independence.[45]

Jay sent back many a letter to Congress despairing of any chance of ever getting Madrid to recognize, let alone ally with, the United States, unless it agreed not only to abandon any notion of Mississippi River navigation, but even territory beyond the Appalachians. Jay declared to Congress that it would be "better for America to have no treaty with Spain than to pursue one on such servile terms."[46]

If that were not discouraging enough, Jay was disgusted by all the duplicity and arrogance pervading the Spanish court. He responded with heartfelt American self-righteousness. To the insistence that he yield on the Mississippi, he angrily replied that the "Americans, almost to a man, believe that God almighty had made that river a highway for the people of the upper country to go to the sea."[47] The uncompromising belief that God sided with America has been a double-edged sword for that nation's foreign policy, then and since.

10

The War for the South:
First Phase

The battle of Monmouth of 1778 was the last large-scale battle in the Northeast. During the next five years, there would be numerous skirmishes and raids, punctuated by several small battles, most notably Gen. Anthony Wayne's capture of 600 redcoats in a surprise night attack at Stony Point on July 15, 1779, and Gen. Henry Lee's capture of 150 redcoats at Paulus Hook on August 19, 1779. Yet neither side was able to break the stalemate. Washington lacked an army powerful enough in troops and cannons to besiege Clinton's army holed up in New York, and Clinton lacked the boldness to march forth and try to run down that elusive fox Washington.

Instead, Clinton shifted the war to the southern states. His plan was to hold New York City and capture Savannah, which would be used as a base to overrun first Georgia and then South Carolina. Next, he would march north. This strategy was premised on word that the South was lightly defended and filled with loyalists yearning to be liberated from rapacious rebel rule.

Lt. Col. Archibald Campbell landed at the head of thirty-five hundred troops near the mouth of the Savannah River on Christmas Day, 1778. A slave led eight hundred light infantry into the city by an unguarded route on December 28. Once inside, the redcoats launched a surprise attack on the eleven hundred American defenders commanded by Gen. Robert Howe, captured or killed nearly six hundred, and routed the rest from the city.

Until Savannah's capture, the war in the southern states had consisted of mostly British and Indian raids and skirmishes between patriots and loyalists.

Nowhere was the civil war between loyalists and patriots more savage and deadly than in the southern states, mainly because they were fairly matched in numbers. It was a seesaw war, in which each side lost and won numerous battles and countless skirmishes. After the British invasion, that vicious but small-scale war would persist, while major campaigns would devastate much of the region, leaving thousands dead and tens of thousands refugees from their looted and burned homes. Some Americans, such as William Moultrie, Francis Marion, and Thomas Sumter, proved to be masters of guerrilla warfare and wore down the British with daring hit-and-run attacks. As for the large-scale fighting, unfortunately, the first three generals who commanded the Southern Department—Robert Howe, Benjamin Lincoln, and Horatio Gates—proved to be utterly inept. Howe was routed from Savannah in December 1778, Lincoln surrendered five thousand troops and the city of Charleston in May 1780, and Gates's army was demolished at Camden in August 1780. It was not until Gen. Nathanael Greene took command in December 1780 that the Americans began what would be a systemic campaign to retake the South.

Gen. Augustine Prevost arrived to take command of the British Army from Campbell in early January 1779 and immediately fanned out expeditions to control much of eastern Georgia. Gen. Benjamin Lincoln had replaced Howe as commander of the Southern Department. With fewer than four thousand troops scattered in various detachments, he mostly sat at his headquarters at Purrysburg, South Carolina, and awaited reinforcements and supplies. At first, as in the North, the southern front stalemated because neither Lincoln nor Prevost had enough troops or determination to launch an attack against the other.

The southern front suffered a devastating blow in May 1779 when a British armada appeared off Hampton, Virginia. Gen. Edward Mathew disembarked at the head of 1800 troops. The handful of American defenders fled without firing a shot. The redcoats swarmed over the port and the fort, burning everything of value. When they reembarked, they had destroyed 2 million pounds sterling worth of provisions and munitions and burned to the waterline or hauled off 137 vessels. Word of the loss of those supplies sharply dampened the morale of the American troops farther south.[48]

The Americans received reinforcements in September 1779 that could have decisively shifted the war and not only in the South. Admiral d'Estaing's experience in New England had been disappointing for him and France's ally. His mission was to aid American independence, but his sailors would mostly be recalled for surviving a devastating hurricane and brawling with local toughs in Boston's taverns and brothels. In early 1779 he ordered his fleet's sails spread for the West

Indies, where he captured the British islands of St. Vincent and Grenada and fought an indecisive naval battle with a British squadron commanded by Cdre. William Hotham on July 6. Then in August orders came that he must hurry back to the United States and help recapture Savannah from the redcoats.

D'Estaing disembarked his three thousand troops near the mouth of the Savannah River on September 13 and linked up with Gen. Lincoln and his army. Prevost, meanwhile, had recalled his garrisons at Sunbury and Port Royal to Savannah. The allied leaders demanded that Prevost surrender. Prevost defiantly refused. D'Estaing had heavy guns from his fleet hauled up and emplaced in siege-works. The guns opened fire on October 4.

Had d'Estaing been patient and conducted a proper siege, Prevost would have eventually been forced to capitulate. He was cut off and outnumbered with no hope of rescue. But once again d'Estaing let down the Americans, this time with disastrous results. He was nervous that a British fleet or another hurricane would ravage his fleet while he, his troops, and many of his sailors were scattered in siege lines around Savannah. He informed Lincoln that he intended to sail away but, before doing so, was willing to join the Americans for a joint assault on the British lines. Lincoln reluctantly agreed.

What ensued was the allied version of Bunker Hill. Of the 3,500 French and 950 Americans who charged the British entrenchments on October 9, more than 700 French and 450 Americans were killed or wounded; the British suffered fewer than 150 casualties. D'Estaing ordered his men and guns returned to his fleet, and he sailed back to the West Indies. Lincoln retreated to Charleston with the rem-nants of his army.

Word of that victory inspired Clinton to launch what he hoped would be a knockout blow against the rebels in the South. He ordered the three thousand troops in Newport to abandon that city and join an armada that would sail to Charleston. The armada began disgorging more than twelve hundred troops near the mouth of Charleston Bay in late February 1780.

Although Lincoln had 2,650 regulars and 2,500 militia in Charleston, he did nothing to resist Clinton's landing or advance. Nor did he try to break out as the redcoats began zigzagging entrenchments and batteries ever closer to the city. To ensure that his siege would not be threatened, Clinton loosened the "British Legion" of fast-moving cavalry and infantry under Lt. Col. Banastre Tarleton against American forces and depots scattered across the South Carolina country-side. The British fleet sailed past the forts guarding the bay, anchored off Charleston, and joined the land batteries in bombarding the city. Lincoln handed over his sword on May 12, 1780.

Lincoln's surrender at Charleston was the worst American defeat of the war. Yet it was far from decisive. After five years of fighting, the war was still a bloody stalemate with no end in sight. In May 1780 the British had more than 37,500 troops in North America but occupied only a few key points. Half those troops were deployed in and around New York City; of those 17,342 men, 7,711 were British, 7,451 were Hessian, and 2,162 were provincials. Of the 12,847 in South Carolina, 7,041 were British, 3,018 were Hessians, and 2,788 were provincials. There were 862 Hessians and 1,016 provincials in Georgia, 3,500 troops in Nova Scotia, 1,400 troops in West Florida, and 536 troops in East Florida.[49]

Before sailing back to New York on June 5, Clinton handed over command of his victorious army to Gen. Edward Cornwallis, with the mission of completing the conquest of the South before marching north to join him. Cornwallis fanned his army out to systematically destroy any rebel forces and capture all key towns and forts across South Carolina and Georgia.

Washington dispatched Gen. Horatio Gates to gather the remnants of the American forces, rebuild them into an army, and march against Cornwallis. Gates did so and advanced with three thousand troops against an arm of the British Army at Camden. Learning of Gates's advance, Cornwallis quick-marched reinforcements to Camden and attacked on August 16, 1780. The result was the latest American rout, with no one fleeing farther than Gates himself, who by nightfall reached Charlotte sixty miles away. The American army was demolished, with more than 1,000 killed or wounded and as many taken prisoner. In contrast, British losses were relatively light, with 69 killed, 245 wounded, and 11 missing.[50]

Camden would be the zenith of Britain's southern campaign. Although they could not have imagined it at the time, during the next three years the Americans would steadily grind down the British Army's men and positions until by the war's end the remnants were holed up in Charleston.

11

Parallel Wars

S pain's influence on the fate of American independence was only slightly less powerful than that of France. Madrid's contributions of money and supplies to the rebels were certainly desperately needed. Yet its military campaigns were even more important because the Spanish captured British colonies and diverted crucial British attention, troops, warships, and supplies from Britain's war against the Americans.

No Spanish commander during the war was more successful than Louisiana governor Bernardo de Galvez. In the three years from 1779 to 1781, he captured the lower Mississippi Valley and the Gulf Coast, and in 1782 he took Bermuda from the British. Elsewhere, the Spanish recaptured Minorca in 1781 and besieged but never retook Gibraltar. Other than Gibraltar, their only setbacks were in joint operations with the French. They massed an armada of sixty-six ships off southeastern England in 1779 but failed to land the army crammed aboard.

The British took advantage of that failure and seized the initiative. Adm. George Rodney sailed forth with his fleet and defeated Admiral Langara's fleet of eleven ships of the line off Cape St. Vincent on January 8, 1780; he sank three, captured four, and scattered the rest. Rodney then sailed for the West Indies. There he engaged the comte de Guichen in indecisive battles off the Leeward Islands in April and May 1780.

Meanwhile, Congress tried every conceivable diplomatic angle to garner support for the revolution. To that end, William Lee was sent to the United Provinces, Austria, Prussia, and the Holy Roman Empire. Although he failed to win unofficial recognition from any of those states, he did inspire offers of mediation by two of history's most remarkable queens. Neither Maria Theresa of Austria nor Catherine of Russia would recognize the independence of the United States, but they were willing to do what they could to bring peace between the Americans and the British. Whitehall politely but firmly declined both offers. That rebuff provoked Catherine into a strong stand against Britain.[51]

There was far more at stake than humanitarian concerns in the widening war that had started with the American revolt. To varying degrees, all the neutral states had suffered as Whitehall tried to sever the rebels from foreign supplies. The admiralty tightened its blockade against the colonies with a series of tougher restrictions against neutral shipping, which allowed its warships and privateers to confiscate cargoes and vessels trading with the Americans. Under an Order in Council issued on November 10, 1778, Whitehall declared that all neutral vessels would be boarded and inspected and those cargoes and vessels bound to or from the rebellious colonies or France would be confiscated.

This naturally enraged neutral states. Vergennes suggested in 1778 that the neutral seafaring states collectively assert their freedom-of-the-sea rights against Britain. Catherine II saw the wisdom in that and had her chief minister, Nikita Ivanovich Panin, propose an alliance to Denmark's foreign minister, Count Andreas Petrus Bernstorff. Although Bernstorff agreed, nothing concrete would appear for two more years. On March 10, 1780, Catherine called for Sweden, Denmark, and the Netherlands to join with Russia in a League of Armed Neutrality dedicated to defending the right of "free ships, free goods," which allowed neutral vessels freely to carry any nonwar supplies to any ports not under blockade. Denmark was the first to accede, signing a treaty with Russia on July 9, followed by Sweden on August 1 and the Netherlands on November 20. Those treaties were combined into one League of Armed Neutrality on January 4, 1781. Eventually, other countries would join, including Prussia on May 19, 1781; Austria on October 9, 1781; the Kingdom of the Two Sicilies on February 21, 1782; and Portugal on July 23, 1782.[52]

The Americans viewed the league's creation as a golden diplomatic opportunity. Congress dispatched Francis Dana of Massachusetts to St. Petersburg with the rather puzzling mission of seeing whether the United States could join. The answer was a curt no, given that the Americans were rebels against Britain and thus neither technically a state nor neutral. Russia's answer did not change during the two years that Dana spent hovering outside the Russian court. The recognition of the United States by Russia and all other league members except the Netherlands would not come until after Britain formally recognized the United States with the 1783 Treaty of Paris.

Meanwhile, the Americans eyed the Netherlands, also known as the United Provinces, as a rich source of loans to help underwrite the war.[53] Only the Dutch financial and mercantile dynamism rivaled that of the British. The empire was small and far-flung, with colonies in several Caribbean islands, Africa's southern Cape, Ceylon, and the East Indies, but it reaped enormous wealth for the Netherlands.

Most Dutch merchants had welcomed the American rebellion as a chance to enter a formerly forbidden market. Yet most officials were more cautious. Dutch naval and economic power had declined precipitously from its height during the seventeenth century. The Dutch understood that any war with Britain would most likely result in the devastation of their trade and the loss of their colonies.

Thus it was in Dutch interests to ally with none and trade with all. The Caribbean colony of St. Eustatius became the key entrepot for trade between the Americans and the Dutch and for military supplies from France to the United States. The Dutch would only recognize American independence and accept an American minister in 1781, after they were convinced that the United States would win.

Congress issued Henry Laurens instructions in October 1779 to journey to the Hague and solicit a Dutch loan. No mission would miscarry as badly. It would be ten months before Laurens set sail on August 13, 1780. A British warship captured his vessel on September 3. Laurens threw a bag of secret documents overboard, but it floated, rather than sank.

What the British found inside would have dire consequences, and not only for Laurens, who was subsequently jailed in the Tower of London. Among the documents fished from the sea was a draft treaty that William Lee had drawn up with Engelbert Van Berckel, who represented a group of Dutch financiers. Neither man was authorized to negotiate a treaty, and that draft was never considered thereafter. They were merely toying with ideas. Whitehall, however, took that document very seriously, at least publicly. On November 10, 1780, Whitehall issued an ultimatum to the Hague to desist from giving any more aid or recognition to the American rebels. The Dutch responded by joining the League on November 20. Nonplussed, George III declared war against the United Provinces on December 20. In doing so, he cited what must rank as among the most pathetic excuses in history, the captured nonofficial document drawn up by nonofficials. The League of Armed Neutrality proved to be a paper tiger. It did not deter Britain from warring against one of its members.

Within a year, the British had captured St. Eustatius, Trincomali, and Ceylon. Yet those victories proved to be costly. By thinning its already thin red line to war against the Dutch, Whitehall further diminished its chances of crushing the American rebellion. And these victories themselves were fleeting. A year later the French would recapture both St. Eustatius and Trincomali.

Meanwhile, Congress dispatched John Adams to join Franklin in Paris and convince the British to grant independence to the United States. Nothing positive came of his peace mission. Adams did not tarry long after reaching Paris on February 9, 1780. Although he was brilliant intellectually, he was not God's gift to diplomacy. The prickly, prudish, vain, proud, and pompous John Adams soon clashed with French minister Vergennes and his minions. Adams saw no way to surmount a French policy designed to "keep us weak. Make us feel our obligations. Impress our minds with a sense of gratitude."[54] The result was a diplomatic brick wall between Adams and his mission. Vergennes curtly informed Adams on July 29 that he wanted no more to do with him; henceforth, he would speak only with Franklin.[55]

Adams had alienated not only the French. Franklin was just as disgusted with him. He wrote Congress a full report of what had happened and hinted that Adams should be recalled.[56]

Adams despaired over what to do. The news that the British had captured Henry Laurens presented an opportunity. Adams decided to take his place as envoy to the United Provinces and lobby for a $10 million loan. He departed Paris for the Hague on July 27. Although he went as a private citizen, on September 16 he got word that Congress had approved his action and issued him a commission to fill Laurens's place.

Adams got along much better with the Dutch than with the French. He found them congenial, down-to-earth, and straight-talking. After all, since the United Provinces was a republic largely run by merchants and financiers, he was dealing with burghers rather than aristocrats—people accustomed to making money and cutting deals. He was in his element.

Still, his mission of securing a $10 million loan, recognition, and an alliance was a grueling uphill diplomatic struggle. It would take him until the autumn of 1782 to win two of those three goals. He would then hurry back to Paris in time to help put the finishing touches on a peace treaty with Britain.

The War for the South: Second Phase

After Camden, the British understandably believed that they could wipe out the remaining American resistance within a few weeks or so. As Cornwallis prepared to march north against the shards of the American army in Charlotte, North Carolina, he sent Maj. Patrick Ferguson and his crack legion of twelve hundred provincials westward into the piedmont to secure that distant flank. But instead of intimidating the "over-mountain" frontiersmen of the western Carolinas, Ferguson's advance kicked in a hornet's nest. The frontiersmen gathered, rode eastward, and caught up to Ferguson and his men at King's Mountain, a low plateau, on October 7. In the ensuing battle, they surrounded the British, picked off Ferguson and 156 others, wounded 163, and captured 689, while 28 were killed and 64 wounded.[57]

Cornwallis's campaign had suffered a sharp, if not decisive, defeat. He redoubled his efforts to march north against the remnants of the American army at Charlotte. Gen. Nathanael Greene had arrived to take command of those troops on December 2, 1780. He had no sooner begun trying to rebuild the army when he learned that Cornwallis was quickly advancing toward him. Greene split his forces, retreating north with eleven hundred troops, while sending Gen. Daniel Morgan with six hundred mostly riflemen northwest on a parallel route that threatened the British flank. Cornwallis took the bait and split his own forces; he pursued Greene with the bulk of his troops and sent Tarleton galloping after Morgan.

Morgan took a carefully chosen stand at Cowpens in western North Carolina. Tarleton caught up with him on January 17, 1781, and immediately attacked with his legion. Morgan executed a near-perfect double envelopment, drawing the British into his center and then overwhelming them on either flank. Tarleton escaped with 200 men to safety but left behind 100 dead and 600 captured; Morgan's victory cost him a mere 12 killed and 60 wounded.[58]

The American victories of King's Mountain and Cowpens destroyed a fifth of Cornwallis's forces and caved in his western flank. Cornwallis sought to redeem those losses with a decisive defeat of Greene. He urged his troops forward in hot pursuit. Greene withdrew toward his supply lines while drawing Cornwallis ever farther away from his.

When Greene judged the time was right, he turned his 4,500 men and stood defiant at Guilford Courthouse. Cornwallis hurled his army against the Americans on March 15, 1781. Although the redcoats held the field by the day's end, they won a Pyrrhic victory. More than a quarter of the British forces, or 554 men, were killed or wounded. Although Greene lost only 227 killed or wounded, more than 1,000, mostly militia, were captured or had deserted. Strategically, Guilford Courthouse was a decisive American victory. Cornwallis withdrew his battered army to Wilmington, North Carolina, and awaited reinforcements and supplies from the British fleet. Aside from the coast, North Carolina was once again securely in American hands.[59]

Rather than pursue Cornwallis, Greene advanced with 1,500 troops south toward Gen. Francis Rawdon and his 900 troops at Camden. Although outnumbered, Rawdon sought to surprise Greene and his men at Hobkirk Hill on April 25. Once again, the British won tactically but lost strategically. The redcoats held the field at the day's end; the losses were about equal, with the Americans and the British, respectively, suffering 271 and 258 dead and wounded. But Greene withdrew his troops a half-dozen miles to another strong position and waited. Rawdon realized his vulnerability and retreated to Charleston.

During the next several months, Greene and his forces mopped up British garrisons at Forts Watson, Motte, Granby, and Orange, taking more than eight hundred men and vast amounts of desperately needed munitions and provisions. The Americans besieged Fort Ninety-Six and the town of Augusta, Georgia. Having received reinforcements, Rawdon marched to the relief of Fort Ninety-Six. Although Greene broke off the siege and retreated, Rawdon recognized the fort's vulnerability and withdrew its garrison with his army eastward.

Cornwallis was well aware that Greene was systematically retaking the Carolinas and Georgia. Yet rather than pursue Greene, Cornwallis pointed his army north and led it to Virginia in a campaign that would abruptly and decisively end at Yorktown.

13

Stalemate, Betrayal, and Mutiny

Meanwhile, the stalemate dragged on in the Northeast. In June 1780 Clinton advanced with most of his army to Springfield, New Jersey. He hoped to provoke Washington to march his army down from their entrenchments around Morristown. Washington equally hoped that Clinton would try to attack him. Both would be disappointed. After a few skirmishes between the advanced guards of both armies, Clinton withdrew to Manhattan.

Washington would soon descend from his stronghold at Morristown after receiving word that on July 11, 1780, a fleet dropped anchor at Newport and disgorged Gen. Jean Baptiste Donatien de Vimeur, the comte de Rochambeau, and the first of eventually fifty-five hundred French troops. Although that was electrifying news, it would take an often-frustrating year of diplomacy before Washington and Rochambeau could agree on just how to work together. The plan they eventually devised would lead to the war's culminating campaign.

Clinton nearly scored a decisive victory against the Americans in 1780, but one of betrayal, rather than combat. Few matched and none surpassed Benedict Arnold in the daring and skill with which he made war. Unfortunately, the flip side of that drive and charisma, which were so inspiring in battle, was an abrasive, domineering, and disdainful personality that alienated others. Arnold had no patience for the haggling, platitudes, and insincerities of politics. He was thus trapped in a vicious political cycle—the more he vented his swelling anger at being passed over for promotions and positions, the more he offended influential congressmen and officers, who in turn abused their power to retaliate against him, which only further fed his rage.

With British major John Andre as a go-between, Arnold began secret negotiations with General Clinton, which led to a deal whereby Arnold would surrender the fortress of West Point, along with George Washington, in return for being made a British general with a field command and 10,000 pounds sterling. He nearly delivered on his promise. He talked Washington into making him commander of West Point and then arranged to have the commanding general and his staff pay a visit.

Arnold and Clinton might have pulled off that plot had not a militia patrol stopped and searched Andre as he tried to slip back to the British lines on September 11, 1780. Finding secret documents, they brought Andre back to the local headquarters for further questioning. On learning of Andre's arrest, Arnold fled across the lines to Clinton's headquarters in New York City. Andre confessed. Washington offered Clinton a trade of Andre for Arnold. Clinton refused. Andre was hanged as a spy. Arnold got his gold, commission, and command.

Although Arnold's betrayal was a crisis, the American army and the cause of independence faced a worsening dilemma. With the continental dollar worth only a penny, rations near starvation levels, and no end to the war in sight, recruitment was scant and desertion was rife. Many hated their officers for meting out harsh punishments for the slightest infractions while enjoying far superior pay, rations, and quarters. To virtually a man, the soldiers despised Congress for being corrupt, inept, and bankrupt and ever more dared voice the near treasonous notion that they might be better off restored to the king's rule.

The Pennsylvania Line, which numbered a quarter of Washington's army, mutinied on New Year's Day, 1781. The troops argued that their three-year terms were done and threatened to go home if they did not immediately receive a reenlistment bonus. The depth of their rage and desperation was unmistakable when they murdered several officers who tried to restore order. Learning of the mutiny, Gen. Henry Clinton sent the Pennsylvanians word that he would pardon and pay them if they switched sides.

Washington and his officers feared that the mutiny would spread like an epidemic through the entire army. They envisioned the troops laying down their arms, marching on Congress, or even eagerly grabbing Clinton's offer. Washington ordered emergency food stores tapped and distributed to the troops and authorized the Pennsylvania's Line's commander, Gen. Anthony Wayne, to meet with the mutiny's leaders. The mutineers now demanded that in addition to a bonus, they could elect new officers and abolish corporal punishment. Wayne promised the creation of a commission that would hear their grievances and recommend reforms, informed them that the Congress they so reviled had voted funds for their immediate relief, and offered them a pardon if they would immediately return to the ranks. The Pennsylvanians accepted.

But these concessions then encouraged the New Jersey brigade to mutiny. This time Washington wielded the stick, rather than the carrot. He ordered reliable regiments to load their muskets, fix bayonets, and surround the New Jersey camp. The New Jersey troops were ordered to parade without arms. Once they had done so, a man was randomly selected from each regiment and executed by a dozen of the mutiny's leaders.

14

Yorktown

Washington had no sooner suppressed the New Jersey mutiny when he learned of another crisis. In December 1780 Clinton had dispatched Arnold with twelve hundred troops to raid Virginia's tidewater region. Arnold's expedition captured Richmond on January 5, destroyed the supply depot, and then withdrew back down the James River to Portsmouth. Virginia was virtually defenseless. Its continental troops were split between the southern and the northeastern fronts. The only significant numbers of armed men left in the state were militia. Washington hurried Marquis de Lafayette and twelve hundred troops to Virginia's rescue in February 1781.

Gen. William Phillips took over command from Arnold on March 30. With reinforcements his army numbered three thousand troops. He tried to chase down Lafayette, but the young general always managed to evade him. Phillips gave up the pursuit and headed toward Petersburg, defeated Friedrich von Steuben and a thousand militia, and captured the town. Von Steuben retreated west up the James River to Point of Fork. Lafayette then hurried his army down to defend Richmond on April 29. Although his army checked Phillips's advance, he would soon have to beat a hasty retreat.

Cornwallis joined Arnold, who had taken command after a fever killed Phillips at Petersburg on May 20. The combined British forces numbered seventy-two hundred crack troops. Splitting his forces, Cornwallis led most of his army north against Lafayette, sent Col. John Simcoe and his Queen's Rangers west against von Steuben, and ordered Tarleton's legion northwest against Charlottesville, where Gov. Thomas Jefferson and the Virginia assembly were meeting. Lafayette and von Steuben managed to escape with their respective forces, while Jefferson and the assembly fled to Winchester in the Shenandoah Valley. Each British column was able to capture large stores of supplies.

Cornwallis ordered his forces to withdraw and meet at Richmond on June 18. After burning what munitions and provisions he could not haul away, Cornwallis marched eastward along the north shore of the James River. He intended to ferry his army across to Portsmouth, where he hoped to rendezvous with a British flotilla that could transport him and his footsore army back to New York.

Lafayette returned to Richmond. After being joined by von Steuben and reinforcements under Gen. Anthony Wayne, his army numbered five thousand troops, although a mere two thousand were continentals. Nonetheless, Lafayette cautiously followed Cornwallis. Tarleton, who was covering the British withdrawal, turned and attacked Wayne, who was leading the American advance, at Green Spring Farm on July 6. Although outnumbered, Wayne ordered his men to charge. That audacious act blunted Tarleton's attack. But the British fed more troops into the battle, and Lafayette finally ordered a withdrawal.

Cornwallis crossed to the south side of the James River to Portsmouth. There he found not a flotilla but orders from Clinton. He was to recross the James River and occupy Yorktown, which would be his base of operations for further campaigns in Virginia. On August 1 he disembarked his army at Yorktown and Gloucester, on the opposite shores of where the York River flows into Chesapeake Bay. Lafayette cautiously marched his army eastward and encamped it at Williamsburg a dozen miles from Yorktown. Inexplicably, Cornwallis ordered his troops to dig in, rather than march against Lafayette.

At this stage of the war, Washington's dream was that the French fleet would bottle up Clinton in New York while the American and French armies jointly besieged him. Washington shared that plan with Rochambeau during their meeting in Wethersfield, Connecticut, from May 21 to 23. Rochambeau countered with a plan to trap Cornwallis in Virginia. The result was a compromise; Rochambeau would march his army from Newport to Washington's camp at White Plains, where they hoped to provoke Clinton into attacking them.[60]

For the next three months, Washington received reports of the cat-and-mouse game between Lafayette and Cornwallis in Virginia and the withdrawal of the British to Yorktown. On August 14 he learned that Adm. Francois Joseph Paul, the comte de Grasse, was sailing with twenty-eight warships toward Chesapeake Bay. With that, Washington agreed to Rochambeau's plan. Leaving a small army to cover New York, Washington and Rochambeau marched their combined forces to Head of Elk, where they boarded a flotilla of vessels and sailed down Chesapeake Bay.

Meanwhile, de Grasse landed three thousand French troops, which joined Lafayette and then sailed back to the entrance of Chesapeake Bay, where he lay in wait for the British. Nineteen British warships under Adm. Samuel Graves arrived on September 5. Both sides cleared the decks and maneuvered to get the wind at their backs. The French got the edge and sailed toward the enemy. Although no ships on either side were immediately sunk, both sides were heavily battered. Darkness brought an end to that day's fighting, as the fleets sailed beyond cannon shot and regrouped as best they could. The French pursued the following day, and the running sea battle raged off and on until September 8, when de Grasse finally ordered his ships to sail back to Chesapeake Bay. The triumph at Yorktown would have been impossible without the French victory at the Capes. On reaching Williamsburg on September 15, Washington began planning for the advance that would besiege Cornwallis. A crisis erupted on September 23 when word arrived from de Grasse that he would soon set sail for the West Indies for the winter. Without a French fleet guarding Chesapeake Bay, the British could rescue Cornwallis, and the great opportunity to bag him would be lost forever. Washington replied with a letter that tapped all his diplomatic and reasoning skills to urge de Grasse to delay his departure several weeks. De Grasse reluctantly agreed to do so.[61]

The American and French armies marched to just beyond cannon shot of Yorktown and began zigzagging entrenchments and batteries forward on September 28. With the excuse that he was outnumbered two to one, Cornwallis decided against launching any spoiling attacks against the enemy. Day after day, the allied guns pounded his men. The crucial battle took place on the night of October 14, when twin French and American bayonet assaults captured two redoubts that covered the British lines; Alexander Hamilton led the American attack.

Cornwallis secretly prepared his army to be rowed across the York River to Gloucester on the night of October 16. Once again, nature favored the American cause. A storm blew in, battered the boats, and made the crossing impossible. The following morning Cornwallis asked for terms. Washington was ready with a reply but for psychological effect did not issue it until the morning of October 18. The British Army would surrender to the Americans and the British flotilla to the French. All troops and sailors would be prisoners for the war's duration. Cornwallis and his senior officers could return to England. Washington gave Cornwallis two hours to agree, or else the bombardment would be resumed. Cornwallis bitterly agreed. With poetic justice, Washington delegated Gen. Benjamin Lincoln, who had surrendered at Charleston, to manage the details of Cornwallis's surrender.

To their dishonor, the British proved to be very bad losers on October 19, 1781. Cornwallis feigned illness, refused to leave his marquee, and sent his second in command, Gen. Charles O'Hara, to carry his sword to Rochambeau rather than to Washington. Rochambeau refused to accept the sword and motioned for O'Hara to carry it to Washington across the road. Washington indicated that Cornwallis's second was to hand his sword to Washington's second, Benjamin Lincoln. Those rather childish British acts only underlined the decisiveness of their defeat. In all, the allies had captured 7,171 soldiers, 1,140 sailors, 191 cannons, 5,000 pounds sterling, and 82 vessels, including 4 frigates.[62] That stunning victory could have been followed by another. Lafayette hurried to de Grasse and urged him to sail to Charleston and blockade that port while the allied armies marched south. De Grasse refused, with the excuse that his orders demanded that he winter in the West Indies. Nonetheless, Yorktown would truly prove to be the beginning of that long war's end.

PART 2

The American Revolution, 1781–1789

What then is this America, this new man?

JEAN DE CREVECOEUR

Novus Ordo Seclorum

"A NEW WORLD NOW BEGINS,"
GREAT SEAL OF THE UNITED STATES

E Pluribus Unum

"FROM MANY ONE,"
GREAT SEAL OF THE UNITED STATES

*The Americans, almost to a man, believe that God almighty
had made that [Mississippi] river a highway for the people
of the upper country to go to the sea.*

JOHN JAY

*Britain has ventured to begin commercial hostilities. I call them hostilities
because their direct object is not so much the increase of their own
wealth, ships, or sailors, as the diminution of ours.*

JOHN ADAMS

A republic, madam, if you can keep it.

BENJAMIN FRANKLIN

15

French Subversion

The Yorktown victory gave the United States enormous potential diplomatic bargaining power.[1] The trouble was that earlier in 1781, Congress had committed a stunning foreign policy flip-flop. The United States had been willing to trade away virtually anything at the diplomatic table in return for official recognition of independence. This included not merely Mississippi River navigation rights to the sea, but even a United States that stretched westward as far as that distant river.

That stance made sense at the time. The war was at a stalemate. The French alliance had so far provided nothing more than disappointments, frustrations, and a disastrous defeat at Savannah. In February 1781 no one could envision that the decisive battle of Yorktown was only eight months away and independence two years beyond that. Perhaps most important, a brilliant salesman appeared to market that minimalist policy in Philadelphia and elsewhere.

French minister Conrad Alexandre Gerard had sailed home in October 1779. For nearly eight more months, the French mission was headed by Francois Barbe-Marbois, the secretary, who kept a low profile. Then, on June 21, 1780, Anne Cesar, the chevalier de La Luzerne, arrived in Philadelphia to fill the post of minister.

Luzerne was a much better diplomat than Gerard had been. Friendly, dashing, and generous, he easily won friends, allies, and admirers. With a mix of charm, logic, and bribes, he soon rallied a majority in Congress and most newspaper editors to his side. His most powerful backer was Robert Livingston, who was then foreign secretary and would be elected president of Congress on August 10, along with Gen. John Sullivan and Princeton president John Witherspoon. Luzerne was as skilled at espionage as he was at politics and diplomacy, although the demands of those pursuits certainly overlap. Somehow he got the ciphers for both John Adams and Henry Laurens. That intelligence gave the French a sharp edge in dealing with the Americans.[2]

As a result, the French essentially controlled American foreign policy during most of 1781 and 1782, at least in Philadelphia. Luzerne all but wrote the 1781 instructions from Congress to the peace mission. Congress dropped the recognition of independence as a precondition for talks, the right to navigate the Mississippi River, and even specific boundaries for the United States. In addition, the commissioners were to cut no deal that violated an existing American commitment, such as the "no separate peace" clause of the alliance treaty with France. Finally, the mission would be subject to French oversight and approval: "You are . . . to undertake nothing in the negotiations for peace or truce without [Versailles's] knowledge and concurrence; and ultimately to govern yourselves by their advice and opinion, endeavoring in your whole conduct to make them sensible how much we rely upon his majesty's influence for effectual aid in everything that may be necessary to the peace, security, and future prosperity of the United States."[3]

So far, John Adams was the only official peace commissioner, and as far as Congress knew, he was still in the Netherlands after French foreign minister Vergennes had declared him persona non grata. Congress decided to dilute Adams's blunt, prickly demeanor within a five-man diplomatic dream team that would also include Benjamin Franklin, John Jay, Henry Laurens, and Thomas Jefferson. But there were some obstacles. Adams was not the only man missing from Paris. Jefferson did not then want to serve. Laurens was a prisoner in the Tower of London. Jay was in Madrid. Only Franklin was in Paris where the negotiations were supposed to take place. Or so they thought.

Actually, Vergennes had recalled Adams to Paris in June 1781, to discuss America's status at a proposed peace conference in Vienna. During July and most of August, Adams and Vergennes exchanged letters on the subject. Adams objected to all of the ideas being floated for Congress, the most important being that the United States would be merely an observer, rather than a participant; that an armistice would be declared; that a peace would be made on *uti possedetis*, or one could keep what one held; and that any peace would be signed with each of the thirteen states separately. Adams insisted that America's independence as thirteen states united into one be recognized, that the United States be accepted as an equal partner in the negotiations, and that Britain must withdraw all of its forces from the United States. Only then would the United States participate in such a conference.[4]

With that exchange, Adams met with his second stalemate in Paris. He returned to the Netherlands, where, on August 26, he learned of the new peace commissioners and instructions. He fired off a protest to Congress, in which he argued that the 1779 instructions best served American interests and rejected any notion that the ends and means of American diplomacy would be subject to the French king's approval.[5]

John Jay was just as appalled when he read the new instructions and learned of Luzerne's role in dictating them. He dashed off his own protest to Congress: "As an American I feel an interest in the dignity of my country, which renders it difficult for me to reconcile myself to the idea of the sovereign independent States of America submitting . . . to be absolutely governed by the advice and opinions of the servants of another sovereign." He foresaw that closing the Mississippi River to American navigation would lead to worsening tensions and even "render a future war with Spain unavoidable."[6]

Yet Jay followed his instructions. On September 22, 1781, he submitted a draft treaty to Foreign Minister Floridablanca by which the United States would relinquish the right to navigate the Mississippi River south of 31 degrees latitude in return for diplomatic recognition, a trade treaty, and an alliance. If Spain spurned the offer, the United States would retain its navigation right to the Mississippi.[7]

Fortunately for American interests, nothing came of Jay's proposed treaty. The concession on the Mississippi River was not enough to satisfy Charles III, Floridablanca, and the other ministers. They wanted nothing less than a United States boxed in between the Appalachians and the Atlantic. With Spain's reconquest of West Florida, they felt that their power was overwhelming and that an American capitulation to their demands was inevitable. They would cling to that position even after learning that a Franco-American army under Washington and Rochambeau had captured Cornwallis and his entire army at Yorktown.

16

The First American Government

nother vital event took place in 1781 that went almost unnoticed. The first "permanent" American government was officially established. It had been a long time coming.

When the delegates of the First Continental Congress agreed to convene a second session on May 10, 1775, the assumption was that it would be as short and intense as the first. In a month or so, if all went well, the delegates would debate and issue their latest position to Parliament, address whatever proposals arose, determine when a third session should convene to ponder Parliament's reply, and then adjourn. It did not turn out that way.

The bloodshed at Lexington and Concord forced Congress into permanent session. The delegates organized themselves into a working government with committees acting like departments for the army, the navy, finance, diplomacy, and relations among the states. Peyton Randolph of Virginia was elected the first president, although he was soon replaced by John Hancock. Each state was allowed one vote in Congress, with nine required to approve procedural issues and unanimity for substantive issues, such as war, diplomacy, finance, and, most memorably, independence.

Some things never change. The Congress of that era was notorious for its factions, animosities, lobbyists, gridlocks, payoffs, and backroom deals, although that dreary litany was occasionally lightened by a stirring speech, a courageous stand, or a creative way to finesse a problem. Of all of the squabbles within Congress and between Congress and the states, the most heated was over money. A deal was struck whereby Congress could raise revenues by printing money and setting tariffs on trade, but only the states could impose taxes.

It was Benjamin Franklin who in July 1775 was the first to propose that Congress convert itself into a permanent national government based on his 1754 "Plan of Union." Congress swiftly shelved that notion. Designing a government would demand an enormous amount of time to debate various versions, forge a consensus over the most appropriate, and approve a final blueprint. After money, arms, and men, time was the most precious commodity; for the present, there was no time to spare.

As Congress began to move inexorably toward declaring independence in 1776, it simultaneously launched an effort to design a permanent government. On June 12 Congress appointed a committee with a delegate from each of the thirteen states to do just that. A mere month later, on July 12, the committee presented its proposal to Congress. The debate raged on and off until August 20, when Congress finally voted to set aside the proposal. Members of Congress had deadlocked bitterly over such issues as slavery, representation, the western territories, taxes, and the confederation's powers. The debate was resumed in April 1777 only after eleven of the thirteen states agreed that sovereignty would remain in the states.

That would be the only agreement for months to come. Along the way, perhaps the most enduring symbolical act of nation making by Congress occurred on June 14, 1777, when it designated the official American flag as "thirteen stripes alternating white and red; that the Union be thirteen stars, white in a blue field, representing a new constellation."[8]

The thirteen delegations voted unanimously to approve America's first constitution, known as the Articles of Confederation, on November 15, 1777. The United States of America would be a confederation of sovereign states. A unicameral Congress with one vote for each state would be the forum for debating and deciding issues that directly or indirectly affected them all. Congress would be empowered to raise an army and a navy but could pay for them only with tariffs or borrowed money. It could request levies of troops and funds from the states proportionate to the population of each. It held the sole power for regulating trade and conducting diplomacy with foreign countries and Indian tribes. Unanimity was required to ratify treaties and amend the Constitution. Otherwise, nine votes were required to approve all other proposals, including a president who would be annually elected. The nascent bureaucracies known as committees were simply renamed boards until 1781, when they were first called departments.

After nearly a year and a half of often acrimonious squabbling on the subject, Congress had done little more than institutionalize its existing arrangements.

While that blueprint might seem modest enough today, it took nearly three-and-a-half years before all the states approved it. The Articles of Confederation did not take effect until Maryland became the last state to ratify it on March 1, 1781.

The following year Congress expressed the American ideal by approving a Great Seal of the United States with two mottoes: Novus Ordo Seclorum (A New World Has Begun) and E Pluribus Unum (Out of Many One). Although there was no question that the Americans had achieved the first motto, the second was, and many would argue remains, a work in process.

Governments are the most obvious expression of national power. Thirteen states fought more or less together for six years before they finally agreed officially to transform a makeshift government into something that at the time they hoped would endure. The new government would last a mere seven years before it was discarded for "a more perfect union."

17

Winning the Peace

The news of Cornwallis's surrender reached Whitehall on November 25, 1781. Lord George Germain, the minister most responsible for directing the war against the rebels, was the first to know. He hurried to Prime Minister Frederick, Lord North, to discuss that disaster's implications. North received that news "as he would have taken a ball in his breast" and then paced back and forth repeating, "O God! It is all over!"[9]

The Yorktown disaster capped a year of mostly defeats in which the British also lost Minorca in the western Mediterranean and the tiny islands of Nevis, St. Kitts, and Montserrat in the Caribbean. Although North asked the king to accept his resignation, George III insisted that he stay. A sacrificial lamb, however, was needed. Gen. Henry Clinton would be recalled and replaced with Gen. Guy Carleton to command British forces in North America. Carleton was instructed to open talks with the Americans for a peace based on home rule by Congress, which would be subordinate to Parliament.

News of the Carleton mission worried Benjamin Franklin, who feared that his war-weary compatriots might be tempted to accept those terms. He fired off a letter to Foreign Secretary Robert Livingston, reminding him that "the King hates us most cordially" and "his character for falsehood and dissimulation is . . . thoroughly known." The Carleton mission will wield every means of "corruption, artifice, and force, until we are reduced to absolute subjection." Thus, "We have no safety but in our own independence."[10]

The growing peace party in Parliament also opposed the Carleton mission but for the opposite reason. The fear was that the Americans would adamantly reject Whitehall's terms, and the debilitating war would continue to grind on. Henry Conway introduced a resolution that called for ending the war simply by granting the United States independence; to the government's disbelief, it passed by nineteen votes on March 4, 1782.

After a couple of weeks of agonizing indecision over what to do, North finally handed the king his resignation on March 4, 1782. The king was so depressed that he considered abdicating and returning to his ancestral home in Hanover. His advisers talked him out of that and instead helped him form a new government led by Charles Watson Wentworth, the marquis of Rockingham, with Charles James Fox as secretary of state for foreign affairs and William Petty Fitzmaurice, the earl of Shelburne, as secretary of state for home and colonial affairs. Although Shelburne was directly responsible for ending the war with the Americans, Fox would wrestle with him for control over that policy. More was at stake than just a turf battle.

Fox and Shelburne differed sharply over what kind of peace best served British interests. As an outspoken liberal, Fox had long sympathized with the Americans and accepted that their independence was inevitable. He favored recognizing that reality as soon and as gracefully as possible and enticing the Americans into an alliance against the French and the Spanish. Shelburne still clung to the delusion that somehow the Americans could be talked into reuniting with the mother country, with Congress subordinate to Parliament.[11]

When Vergennes learned that Guy Carleton was authorized to open peace talks with the Americans, he fired off a letter to Luzerne calling on him to assert all of his power to prevent that. Even without Luzerne's pressure, Congress most likely would have spurned Carleton's offer, just as it had the Carlisle commission back in 1778. Regardless, Vergennes believed that he could control any talks that took place in Paris. In that, he would be mistaken. Holding the talks in Paris may have actually worked to America's advantage. The diplomats could work without anxious congressmen, lobby groups, or journalists breathing down their necks. The two months or so that letters took to travel between Philadelphia and Paris deterred congressional micromanagement and buffered the diplomats from volatile shifts of public opinion. And most important, Vergennes did not reckon on the American commissioners spurning their own instructions from Congress.

The passage of Conway's peace resolution provided the perfect diplomatic opening for Benjamin Franklin. He sent a note to Shelburne on March 21, 1782, suggesting that the time had come to end the war. When he did so, he believed that Shelburne was still an influential opposition member of Parliament who also wanted peace now. Although rumors had predicted North's fall, Franklin had no idea that Shelburne would soon accept the portfolio of secretary for home and colonial affairs.[12] Franklin's friendly letter could not have been a more welcome gift to Shelburne as he took up his ministry's duties. But just how serious was Franklin? Shelburne dispatched Richard Oswald to find out.

Franklin warmly welcomed Oswald into his home at Passy on April 12. The two were old friends from Franklin's years as a colonial agent in London. On April 17 they paid a visit to Vergennes and explained their intention to talk. Vergennes approved but warned against any separate peace. As Oswald prepared to depart with his report for London, Franklin suggested that the subsequent negotiations could be swiftly concluded if Britain promised to cede Canada to the United States.[13]

The Rockingham cabinet decided on April 23 to return Oswald to Paris for more informal talks with Franklin. As a conciliatory gesture, accompanying Shelburne was Henry Laurens, who had spent most of the previous year incarcerated in the Tower of London. The two journeyed first to the Netherlands, where Laurens met with Johns Adams in Haarlem on May 15. Because Laurens was on parole, Adams refused to reveal any details of his latest congressional instructions. Laurens was too broken in health and spirit to press the issue. He would recuperate in the Netherlands until the eve of the treaty's signing.

Oswald reappeared in Paris on May 4. Franklin was disappointed to learn that Oswald brought with him no formal powers to negotiate but was merely authorized to talk informally about the outlines of a possible peace. Nonetheless, they began a series of discussions that would culminate in a peace treaty nearly seven months later.

During Oswald's visit on May 8, he brought a young companion. Not to be outdone by Shelburne, Fox had tapped Thomas Grenville as his own peace envoy. The choice was ironic. Grenville's father had authored the Stamp Act that kicked off the decade of worsening American protests and resistance, which culminated with the gunfire on Lexington's green. Fox had sent Grenville to Paris ostensibly to see whether Vergennes was amenable to talks, but he hoped to position Grenville so that he would be part of a negotiating team, if and when the cabinet got around to designating one. Franklin introduced Grenville to Vergennes, who said he would welcome any talks.

Oswald and Grenville carried that invitation back to London. On May 23 the cabinet agreed that the two envoys could begin formal peace talks. After the envoys returned to Paris, Grenville sought out Franklin for a private meeting on

June 1. What he revealed was astonishing. He was not only empowered to nego-tiate peace with the United States, but could also recognize America's uncondi-tional independence before talks even began.

Franklin could see the difference in style but not in substance between Fox and Shelburne and their respective envoys. Propriety trumped pragmatism; having begun talks with his letter to Shelburne, Franklin could not bring himself now to spurn him for his political rival. Finally, Franklin preferred talks with his old friend, the elderly but dignified and learned Oswald, over the younger, brash, and slightly disdainful Grenville. Yet in doing so, Franklin unwittingly lost a chance for the quicker and more generous peace that Grenville would have offered.

Despite that notable lapse, Franklin's grand strategy was sound enough. He ex-plained that "the true political interest of America . . . in observing and fulfilling the engagement, with greatest exactitude, the engagement of our alliance with France, and behaving at the same time toward England so as not entirely to ex-tinguish her hopes of a reconciliation."[14]

Keeping true to the alliance, while seeking peace on American terms with Britain, was a very delicate balancing act. Eventually, Franklin and his colleagues would pull off a brilliant deal, partly by playing their ally and their enemy against each other. The key was to separate the American and the French talks with Britain, while getting Vergennes to approve whatever the Americans won. Meanwhile, Shelburne and Fox alike were especially concerned to learn "what our obligations were and how far they extended" to France, now and after the war. Franklin was adept at sidestepping such questions while hinting that the United States might be willing to end the alliance if Britain would offer a generous peace.[15]

The alliance had recently suffered a sharp blow. Word arrived in late May that on April 12, 1782, a British fleet commanded by George Rodney had devastated a French fleet under Francois Joseph Paul de Grasse at the Battle of the Saintes, a small group of islands south of Guadeloupe, sinking seven warships and captur-ing the admiral himself. That not only thwarted a planned French and Spanish at-tack on Jamaica but completely shifted the naval power balance in the Caribbean. That victory would stiffen Britain's sagging diplomatic backbone, at least for a while.

After Oswald's initial visit in April, Franklin felt in need of a colleague to act as the diplomatic bad cop to his own good cop approach. In late April he wrote to John Jay, imploring Jay to join him as soon as possible. With enormous relief, Jay finally departed Madrid for Paris in May 1782. There he would assist Franklin in negotiating a peace with the British while conducting talks for an alliance with

Spain with its minister, Count Aranda. John Jay reached Paris on June 23 but had no sooner joined Franklin in separate talks with the French and the British when influenza laid him up for several weeks.

The tug-of-war between Shelburne and Fox over what kind of peace to forge with the Americans was resolved on July 1, when Rockingham died of the same influenza epidemic that had sickened Jay. The king elevated Shelburne to chief minister, Thomas Townshend to the secretary of state for home and colonial affairs, and Thomas Robinson, Lord Grantham, as secretary for foreign affairs. Grenville resigned after learning that his mentor Fox was back in the House of Commons. That left Oswald in sole charge of talks with the Americans. Grantham dispatched Allyne Fitzherbert to replace Grenville. Fitzherbert would conduct parallel and at times overlapping talks with the French and the Spanish. The two envoys reported to different bosses, Oswald to Home Secretary Townsend and Fitzherbert to Foreign Secretary Grantham. Fearing that the good-hearted Oswald might be too conciliatory to stand firm on British interests, Shelburne tapped David Hartley and Benjamin Vaughan to open unofficial back channels with the Americans.

Nonplussed by the news, Franklin ratcheted up the talks on July 10 by submitting a list of "necessary" and "advisable" terms for peace. To no one's surprise, independence topped the necessary list; Britain must officially recognize American sovereignty even before a treaty was signed. Any treaty must include ample American boundaries and Newfoundland fishing rights. Franklin touted his advisable list as a way to reconcile relations between Americans and Britons. That would come only if Whitehall conceded all of Canada, accepted free trade between the United States and Britain, compensated those whose property had been destroyed by British depredations, and acknowledged the "error in distressing those countries so much as we have done." As for that last request, Franklin most likely smiled wryly as he explained that "a few words of that kind . . . would do more good than people could imagine."[16]

With those lists, Franklin strayed off the diplomatic reservation in several ways. He discarded that year's congressional instructions that the envoys submit their diplomatic strategy and goals to French control. Instead, Franklin told Vergennes only what he already knew: that he was meeting with Oswald. He revealed nothing about the nature of their talks. Eventually, he and his colleagues would violate both the letter and the spirit of the 1778 alliance that forbade no separate peace. But Franklin also committed an elementary diplomatic mistake by revealing his full hand so early in the game. That let the British ignore the "advisable" requests and concentrate on negotiating away the "necessary." Franklin never explained why he did not list all of his demands as necessary and then bargain away such nonessentials as a prior recognition of independence or the admission of British guilt. Indeed, he never revealed his ploy in writing. It was Oswald who recorded Franklin's lists and sent them off to London.

Shelburne replied with a blunt rejection of the necessary and advisable lists alike. On August 6 Oswald read Shelburne's latest instructions. The only acceptable peace would include a political union between Americans and Britons in which Congress was subordinate to Parliament, American debts would be paid in full to their British creditors, and loyalists would be fully compensated for the property destroyed or stolen by the rebels. Oswald also received an unsigned commission that empowered him to negotiate peace with any envoys "named by the said colonies and plantations." There was pointedly no mention, let alone recognition, of the United States. After Oswald showed his commission to Franklin and Jay, who had recovered from the flu, a dispute erupted that would distort the talks and delay a settlement.

It was at that time that the American diplomatic strategy was transformed into a sort of tag-team, good cop/bad cop routine. Jay insisted to Franklin that they break off talks with Oswald unless Whitehall rewrote his commission in a way that recognized American independence. Vergennes, with whom Franklin and Jay met on August 10, wisely urged them to set aside recognition for the final treaty and concentrate on the key issues for now. But Jay convinced a reluctant Franklin to hold firm not only against the British but also against the French. They would defy their 1781 instructions from Congress to let Vergennes control their diplomacy and, if necessary, sacrifice any other national interests for the sake of independence. Instead, they would win a peace based on the 1779 instructions.[17]

After a painful kidney stone forced Franklin to drop out for several weeks, Jay and Oswald squared off alone across the diplomatic table. Jay added clarity to Franklin's insistence on generous American boundaries. The United States would extend to the Mississippi River, and Americans would have the right to freely navigate that river to the sea. To strengthen his hand, he hinted that the United States was negotiating with Spain and Holland for alliances, and if those were consummated, the Americas would undoubtedly demand more concessions. Oswald found this credible because Jay was also closeting himself with Spanish minister Aranda, while Adams was in the United Provinces negotiating with the Dutch.

Jay's tough line worked. Shelburne and his cabinet were willing to accept all of Franklin's "necessary" demands, but they felt that they needed parliamentary approval for such a powerful symbolic step, and the members were in recess and would not return for several months. Oswald was instructed to negotiate away those demands "only in the very last resort" if the Americans yielded on the other key issues.[18]

Here was yet another golden diplomatic opportunity that an American diplomat failed to uncover and act on. Jay remained in the dark over how much negotiating latitude Oswald had received. Meanwhile, Aranda stood firm on the same demands that Jay had heard for nearly two years in Spain. Recognition and an alliance would be considered only if the Americans gave up claims to most land west of the Appalachians and navigation on the Mississippi River.

So Jay, who had been so adamant on recognition, did not stick to his guns on other "necessary" issues. He began to backpedal on both the Newfoundland fisheries and the Mississippi River. He even went so far as to encourage the British to reconquer Pensacola and the rest of West Florida from the Spanish: "What are you doing with twenty thousand men? Why don't you ship them from Charleston and New York and seize West Florida?"[19] This was self-serving advice, whether or not the United States and Spain really were on the verge of allying, as Jay had earlier hinted.

Yet the best explanation is Jay's deepening distrust of the French and the Spanish. During nearly two and a half years of mostly diplomatic isolation in Madrid, he had acquired an ill-concealed loathing for European duplicity. Now in Paris, he channeled that animosity against both Vergennes and Aranda. He believed that they were trying to prolong the war and manipulate the Americans. He explained the essence of French policy: "They are interested in separating us from Great Britain and on that point we may, I believe, depend upon them; but it is not their interest that we become a great and formidable people, and therefore they will not help us to become so." As for the Spanish, they completely opposed American independence.[20]

Aranda's position on the boundary would shock the proud envoy from the new republic. The Spaniard rejected both the Mississippi navigation and the 31st degree latitude frontier, and he also demanded a line drawn from Georgia's southern boundary northward to Lake Erie's western shore. To Jay, that was not only unacceptable—it was insulting. After calming down, he turned to Vergennes for help. Vergennes backed Spain's interest in containing the United States as far east as possible. To that end, he assigned his secretary, Joseph Mathias Gerard de Rayneval, to work with Aranda to draw a line acceptable to France and Spain. What they contrived zigzagged its way from Georgia to the Ohio River, leaving an American frontier on the Mississippi only from the Ohio River's mouth northward. Jay disdainfully rejected that proposal as well.

Fitzherbert's talks with the French and the Spanish got a boost in August after Shelburne paroled de Grasse and sent him to Paris with a sweeping peace proposal. Whitehall would grant independence to the United States; allow Spain to keep West Florida and Minorca or Gibraltar; restore to France St. Lucia, Dominica, its former possessions in India, and fishing rights off eastern Canada; and root a peace with the United Provinces on *uti possedetis*, or each could keep what it had taken.

Vergennes sent Rayneval off to London for direct talks with Shelburne. The two first met on September 13. With the "no separate peace" clause embedded in the Franco-Spanish alliance, any deal that they cut depended on Madrid's approval. Vergennes corresponded with Floridablanca over whether the time was right for ending the war and, if so, on what terms.

Jay's distrust deepened when he learned of Rayneval's departure and destination on September 9. Would the French and the British cut a secret deal against the United States that severed it from the Mississippi? It was fear of collusion between America's ally and enemy that prompted Jay to reverse himself on the issue that he believed was so important. He told Oswald that he would accept a carefully worded document that implicitly, rather than officially, recognized American independence. He then tried to convince Oswald that it was in British interests to accept a United States that stretched westward to the Mississippi River. Finally, Jay talked Benjamin Vaughan into hurrying to London and pressing Shelburne to spurn a deal with the French and instead settle with the United States; as a sweetener, he renounced any American claims to Canada north of the Great Lakes.

Oswald's latest commission arrived in Paris on September 27. To Jay's delight, the document was artfully composed to empower Oswald to "treat with the Commissioners appointed by the Colonies, under the title of Thirteen United States, inasmuch as the Commissioners have offered under that condition to accept the independence of America as the First Article of the Treaty."[21]

With that done, the pace of the talks quickened. On October 5 Jay submitted a draft treaty that included the necessary items on Franklin's list. The boundaries were based on the instructions Congress had penned to Adams on August 14, 1779.

The timing was unfortunate. Whitehall learned on September 30 that Gibraltar's defenders had bloodily repulsed a Spanish assault on September 13. Shortly thereafter, a supply convoy succeeded in breaking through the Spanish blockade and unloading in Gibraltar. Although the siege continued, clearly the Spanish would be unable to capture the Rock.

That siege had lurked as the ghost at the cabinet's policy table during most of the summer. With that threat gone, the British could afford to take a harder line. Correspondingly, after its humiliating defeat, Madrid grudgingly agreed to follow the lead of the Americans and the French by negotiating peace with the British.

Jay had squandered weeks of valuable time over the recognition issue when Gibraltar's siege made the British more susceptible to compromise.

The cabinet received Jay's draft treaty on October 11. After six days of debate, the ministers agreed to issue a new set of instructions to Oswald. Peace must be based on compensation to loyalists and creditors and denial of any access right to Newfoundland's fisheries. The British would, however, accept a United States largely based on Jay's proposal, along with Mississippi River navigation rights. Shelburne dispatched Henry Strachey to carry those latest instructions to Oswald and assist him in negotiating them.

After receiving an urgent summons from Jay dated September 28, John Adams put the finishing touches on his diplomacy with the Netherlands and reached Paris on October 26. His diplomacy had been as skilled in the Hague as it had been inept in Paris. The Dutch formally recognized the United States on April 19, 1782. Adams cut a deal on June 11, 1782, with a consortium of Dutch bankers for a 5 million guilder loan at a 5 percent interest rate. Finally, Adams signed a commercial treaty modeled on the "Plan of 1776" with the United Provinces on October 8, 1782. In all, although the United Provinces did not formally ally with the United States, the Dutch had agreed to aid, trade, and recognition.

The latest round began on October 29, when Oswald and Strachey met with Jay, Franklin, and Adams. In day after day of often grueling haggling, the diplomats decided one issue after another. Now Adams joined Jay as bad cops to Franklin's good cop; they rejected any notion of compensation to loyalists or creditors. Eventually, the Americans would give in on those issues. The British in turn yielded on the fisheries, eventually agreeing that the Americans would enjoy the "right" to fish the Newfoundland Banks and the "liberty" to dry their catch on uninhabited shores. As for the boundaries, they finally accepted a United States that ran up the St. Croix River to its headwaters and westward to the St. Lawrence River; then up the center of Lakes Ontario, Erie, Huron, and Superior; then westward to Lake of the Woods and the Mississippi River's source, down the Mississippi to the 31st parallel, and over to the Apalachicola River.

By November 29 the peacemakers had written up all of the agreements into a draft treaty that they intended to sign the next day. At that point, Henry Laurens appeared. Although he had played no role in the negotiations, his colleagues would urge that martyr of American diplomacy to sign the treaty. While Laurens's presence added poignancy to the proceedings, at least for the Americans, something far more important occurred on November 29.

America's alliance treaty with France gave Versailles veto power over any deal that the United States struck with Britain. A separate peace was explicitly forbidden.

Yet that was what the Americans essentially were doing, albeit with implicit French approval. Franklin had periodically informed Vergennes of what was transpiring. For his part, Vergennes was not surprised—spies had already informed him of many details—nor did he begrudge those American efforts.

So Vergennes was not shocked when he received a note from Franklin on the evening of November 29, informing him that a preliminary treaty would be signed the following day. Indeed, he was secretly pleased. The war had gone on long enough. The French and the Spanish had won most of their goals. The time for peace had come. Yet for diplomatic effect, he would feign an anger he did not feel. He could always blame American perfidy for getting France off the hook of further obligations to Spain.[22]

The American and British diplomats gathered at Oswald's residence at the Grand Hotel Muscovite on November 30. Franklin, Jay, Adams, and Laurens signed for the United States and Oswald for Britain. They then celebrated with a grand feast at Franklin's home in Passy.

Even with the Americans essentially out of the game and the French reluctant to continue, the Spanish were determined to keep fighting. Their failure at Gibraltar spurred them to launch a knockout blow against the British. Madrid placed its bet on a planned joint Spanish and French armada massing at Cadiz to sail against Jamaica. Versailles was getting cold feet, however, and gently insisted that it was time to end the war. It was not until December that Madrid finally gave way and began to discuss a common negotiating position with Versailles against the British.

It took another seven weeks of hard bargaining before the British signed separate preliminary treaties with the French and the Spanish on January 20, 1783. France would regain the Caribbean islands of St. Lucia and Dominica, slave depots in Senegal and Gambia, Pondicherry in India, and Pierre and Miquelon off the Newfoundland Banks, where fish could be dried. Those were paltry gains for an investment of more than a billion livres.[23] But the British would get even less—the tiny islands of Nevis, St. Kitts, Tobago, Grenada, and St. Vincent. Spain would gain the Floridas and Minorca but not Gibraltar, its supreme war goal. British woodcutting in the Spanish Empire would be confined to the Honduras coast between the Belize and Hondo rivers. The British included the Dutch in the general armistice, even though they had yet to cut a deal.

Although the guns had finally fallen silent, a genuine peace was still a long way off. That carefully contrived set of agreements appeared to be no more than a precarious house of cards when the House of Commons censured Shelburne's policies on February 22, 1783. Shelburne resigned two days later. The king accepted a coalition government led again by those strange bedfellows of ideology and personality, Frederick North and Charles Fox, with William Henry Cavendish Bentinck, the duke of Portland, acting as the cabinet's figurehead. Rather than sweep clear the diplomatic table and start fresh, the cabinet agreed to accept the broad outlines of the existing agreements, while tinkering with the more objectionable details.

Astonishingly, not everyone in Congress and beyond was pleased when they read the preliminary draft. Robert Livingston, the foreign affairs secretary and a likely recipient of French donations, condemned the commissioners for exceeding their authority. Others in the French party echoed Livingston's criticism. Yet those stern voices were drowned out by the overwhelming cheers for the peace that had been won.

The Americans and the British signed the definitive Treaty of Paris at the Hotel d'York on September 3, 1783, with Benjamin Franklin, John Jay, and John Adams representing the United States, and David Hartley, Britain.

The definitive treaty differed from its predecessor only in minor clarifications. Under the first tenet, Britain granted unconditional recognition of and "perpetual peace" with the United States, although as a confederation of thirteen "free, sovereign, and independent States." The boundaries of those United States would run from the St. Croix River to its source, then eastward along the watershed to the Connecticut River, down that river to the 45-degree latitude, westward to the Iroquois or Cataray River, north down it to the St. Lawrence, and then up that river to Lake Ontario, which, along with Lake Erie, the Detroit River, Lake Huron, and Lake Superior, would be equally divided; then westward from Lake Superior to Lake of the Woods and then the Mississippi River headwaters, down that river to 31 degrees latitude, then eastward to the Apalachicola River, down that river to the Flint River, then eastward to the St. Mary's River, and down it to the Atlantic Ocean.

The treaty then addressed a list of issues. Americans were granted the right to fish off the Newfoundland Banks, in the mouth of St. Lawrence Bay, and in other traditional fishing grounds and could dry their catch where they had previously done so. Creditors on either side would not be impeded from seeking to recover debts. Congress would encourage the states to allow the restoration of property that had been confiscated from loyalists and to prevent any future confiscations. All prisoners of war would be released. Britain would evacuate all American territory and forts and restore all property and documents "with all convenient speed." The Mississippi River "from its source to the Ocean shall forever remain free" to Americans and British alike.

That peace and the terms that bound it would not become official until ratifications were exchanged in Paris on May 12, 1784. While nearly all of the treaty's tenets would be disputed in the years and the decades ahead, one could not be doubted—the United States had won official recognition of its independence.

18

Why America Won

The Americans won independence because they eventually matched or exceeded the British in every vital source of power—military, economic, political, diplomatic, and moral.

Credit must first go to the men who joined the ranks and fought the British under the most wretched conditions. During eighty months of war, more than 217,000 men, or 5.7 percent of the 3.5 million total population, served in America's military forces. Those men suffered 4,435 killed in action, including 4,044 soldiers, 432 sailors, and 49 marines. There were also 6,188 wounded, including 6,004 soldiers, 114 sailors, and 70 marines. Disease killed as many as 25,000 other American soldiers, including 8,000 who died as British prisoners of war.[24]

Aside from the courage of those who fought, America's military power was beset by an array of weaknesses whose primary flaw was leadership. Any analysis of military leadership must start at the top. The inescapable reality is that Washington lost far more battles than he won. He suffered three faults as a field general, which he eventually overcame. First, he frequently failed to send out enough scouts and spies to properly reconnoiter the countryside and figure out just where the enemy troops were located and what they intended. Second, at times he neglected to secure his flanks, which led to the debacles of Brooklyn Heights and Brandywine. Finally, he kept a loose rein over his command structure. A more hands-on commander could have turned the defeat at Germantown and the draw at Monmouth into decisive victories.

Yet generalship is more than fighting battles. No one exceeded Washington in his day-to-day management of the army and his mastery of the countless details that kept his men fed, clothed, armed, trained, disciplined, and spirited as best as was possible under nearly impossible conditions. And his leadership went beyond that. With his indomitable will, a gravitas that commanded all those around him, his burst of strategic creativity that animated the Trenton and Princeton campaigns, and his undying devotion to his country, George Washington came to embody the American Revolution. It is certainly unlikely that the United States would have won independence when and how it did without George Washington in command of the army.

Beyond Washington, America's generals were a very mixed bag. The army was saddled with some generals who at best were mediocrities and who often were outright incompetent, such as Horatio Gates, Charles Lee, Israel Putnam, Arthur St. Clair, and Benjamin Lincoln. Judged by their mastery of strategy, tactics, and command on and off the field of battle, the Americans had at least four excellent generals: Daniel Morgan, Benedict Arnold, Nathanael Greene, and John Stark, and possibly a fifth, Richard Montgomery, although he was killed before he could reveal the array of his abilities. Then there were such daring and skilled leaders as George Rogers Clark, Francis Marion, Thomas Sumter, and Andrew Pickens, who rarely led more than a couple of hundred men but had mastered guerrilla warfare and repeatedly defeated the British in mostly small-scale combats. Three generals rank somewhere in between the gifted and the inept. Neither John Sullivan nor Lafayette ever displayed any creativity, let alone brilliance, as generals but were solidly dependable and deserve high marks for how each, respectively, conducted the 1779 campaign against the Iroquois and the 1781 campaign in Virginia. Anthony Wayne certainly gets mixed reviews. He was ruthlessly brilliant at Stony Point and Green Spring Farm, but his failure to reconnoiter the countryside or even post enough pickets at Paoli led to a devastating defeat. And what does it say about his leadership skills that his troops nicknamed him "Mad Anthony" and mutinied several times?

As for Congress, the essential trouble was that there were too few Americans and too many nationalists from each state. What followed, more often than not, was gridlock, along with inefficiency and corruption. The states imposed crippling restrictions on Congress, the worst of which was the inability to tax. As a result, Congress either printed or borrowed money, which led to a worthless currency, soaring prices, and a deepening debt to foreign creditors. The nadir of American political power came in 1781, when French minister Luzerne manipulated Congress into mistaking French for American interests. Congress issued instructions to its envoys in Paris to sacrifice any other American interests necessary to win independence.

During the decade leading up to the war and during the war itself, the Americans tried to wield market power against Whitehall. Then and for several generations thereafter, most believed that they could bring Britain to its knees simply by denying it products or purchases. The trade cutoff did hurt Britain—exports dropped 15 percent from 1776 to 1782. That may not seem like much, but the loss of those markets, higher insurance costs and taxes, and privateer depredations bankrupted scores of firms and devastated countless others. Merchants and financiers were among Britain's most vociferous advocates of peace.[25]

Only diplomacy could break the military stalemate. Yet diplomacy was as much a skill to be learned and ideally mastered as any other element of power. Although Benjamin Franklin, Arthur Lee, and several others had served as colonial agents in London before 1775, all the Americans were novices at power politics when the war broke out. Most proved to be quick learners.

In mastering the art of diplomacy, the Americans had to overcome their own cultural values rooted in such republican virtues as candor, reason, and simplicity. Many experienced culture shock at the unashamed decadence, lethargy, artifice, frivolity, and falsehood that abounded in Europe's courts and ministries. That is not to say that the Americans were always paragons of virtue. The notion of conflict of interest was blurry in the eighteenth century. Indeed, those in power were expected to advance public and private interests. Yet as Silas Deane found out, American political culture did have a corruption threshold. Deane was recalled from Paris for mingling his official and private accounts.

Overall, no one was more adept at diplomacy than Benjamin Franklin. He was the ideal choice for America's envoy to France, having already spent fifteen years, from 1757 to 1762 and 1764 to 1775, as a colonial agent in London. With his charm, wit, learning, and array of achievements in philosophy, science, journalism, and statesmanship, he epitomized the Enlightenment, and most of the French elite adored him. Arthur Lee, John Adams, and John Jay also deserve high marks for their diplomatic skills and accomplishments. The 1778 treaties of alliance and trade with France and the 1783 peace treaty with Britain were outstanding, if flawed, triumphs of American diplomatic power.

The American will to fight ultimately proved more powerful than that of the British. The Americans suffered devastating defeats at Quebec, Brooklyn Heights, Fort Washington, Brandywine, Savannah, Charleston, and Camden, to name the more prominent. At times the armies dwindled in number, provisions, and morale to the point where they appeared ready to completely dissolve, and with them the

American cause. The Americans, however, were fighting not only for abstract political ideals, but for their livelihoods, homes, and pride. And that kept enough of them in the fight until they ultimately prevailed.

At the same time, the confidence and determination of the British government and public to crush the rebellion were steadily ground down by year after year of bloody stalemate and soaring national debt, punctuated by a series of sharp, humiliating blows that included the defeats at Concord, Bunker Hill, Trenton, Princeton, and Guilford Courthouse, capped by the decisive loss of entire armies at Saratoga and Yorktown. Ever more people, especially merchants whose fortunes were ruined by the war, wanted the fighting to end. That swelling opposition, however, was never expressed through public protests. Instead, people voiced their antiwar sentiments through grumblings in taverns and counting houses, private pleas by powerful lobby groups to politicians, and speeches in Parliament. The Gordon Riots of June 1780, in which more than 250 people were killed and hundreds more were wounded, were not necessarily against the war. Those riots were initiated by Lord George Gordon, who formed the Protestant Association and led a march on Parliament in protest against the Catholic Relief Act of 1778. Yet they reflected a worsening frustration at Whitehall and its policies. Parliament finally threw in the towel with the Conway Resolution of February 1782. Thereafter, it was up to the cabinet to accept American independence with the best deal possible.

It is rarely noted in American history books that the same day that the British signed the Treaty of Paris with the United States, they also signed definitive peace treaties with the French and the Spanish and a preliminary agreement with the Dutch. It was appropriate that Whitehall concluded peace on the same day with all of Britain's enemies. It is certainly a reminder that the history of each would have differed sharply had they not all fought against Britain. Certainly, American independence would have been impossible at that time without massive foreign aid, the direct alliance with France, and the parallel alliances with Spain and the Netherlands.

Most Americans who wanted independence preferred having others pay for it. For a variety of self-interested reasons, those foreign creditors were eager to oblige. French and Spanish financial aid was vital for keeping alive the American cause. The exact amounts will never be known. By one count, France handed out $1,996,500 in grants and $6,352,500 in loans, compared to Spain's $397,230 in grants and $238,098 in loans. Another calculation found that by 1780, Versailles had given the United States 6 million livres, plus an 8 million livres loan for which interest was delayed until after the war ended. It then gave Congress 6 million livres during each of the three years from 1780 to 1782 and expended another 16 million livres on French army and navy forces in the United States. In all, the

French contributed 48 million livres in financial aid to America's war for independence.[26] Those numbers only partly covered the payments for all the shiploads of arms and munitions that unloaded in American ports.

Of course, France contributed not just treasury but blood to America's independence struggle. In all, more than twelve thousand French troops served in the United States during the war, while other expeditions fought elsewhere against Britain. Yorktown would never have happened had Admiral d'Estaing lost the Battle of the Capes or Washington not agreed to Rochambeau's plan to march south against Cornwallis.

Yet those decisive victories obscure the broader relationship. It was not an alliance made in heaven. Communication between the Americans and the French was poor; coordination was worse. Had Admiral d'Estaing conducted a methodical siege at Savannah in 1780, the allies could have bagged a significant number of British troops; instead, his impatience led to a bloody defeat. Rochambeau's army disembarked at Newport, Rhode Island, in July 1780 and holed up there for eleven months while Cornwallis was rampaging through the Carolinas.

The Battle of the Capes and Yorktown aside, the most important role of the allied armies and navies was to distract and divert British military power from the United States to other parts of the world. In that, allied naval power was crucial. As such, American independence was as much won at sea as on land. The distribution of naval power shifted steadily in America's favor.[27] Although during the war the Americans never manned a warship larger than thirty guns, the number of foreign ships of the line with fifty or more guns arrayed against Britain steadily increased and eventually outnumbered those of the Royal Navy.

TABLE 1

Year	France	Spain	Netherlands	United States	Allied	Britain
1778	52	—	—	0	52	66
1779	63	58	—	0	121	90
1780	69	48	—	0	117	95
1781	70	54	13	0	137	94
1782	73	54	19	0	146	94

Of course, numbers tell nothing about how all those warships were deployed, manned, and captained. The British persisted in outsailing and outfighting the allies on nearly all occasions. Yet what was essential was that the more sailors and soldiers the British were forced to bring against the French, the Spanish, and the Dutch, the fewer they could concentrate against the Americans.

19

American Interests and Power in a "World Turned Upside Down"

The war shifted the international distribution of power. The only clear winners were the United States, which gained independence, and Spain, which regained the Floridas and Minorca. Likewise, the only clear loser was the Netherlands, which lost Ceylon. But just what Britain and France gained or lost is more ambiguous and would have profound consequences for American interests, power, and policies through 1815.

In first secretly aiding and then openly allying with the United States, Foreign Minister Vergennes was merely promoting French interests as he saw them. The American rebellion appeared to be a godsend for France. By aiding the rebels, France could bleed British power, wealth, and prestige; the British Empire would suffer a devastating blow if the Americans actually won independence. That in turn would at once partly avenge and compensate France for the losses suffered by the 1763 Treaty of Paris, which ended the Seven Years' War.

Yet Vergennes failed in how he tried to take advantage of the rebellion. Essentially, he did not reckon on several forces that would limit French gains and British losses from the American war. The most vital was the ultimately self-destructive cost of French financial and military aid. France's eventual bankruptcy would lead to not one but two revolutions, one in America and the other in France. Finance Minister Turgot had warned that piling up the national debt would lead to catastrophic results, but Vergennes, the king, and the other ministers, who supported first secret aid and then open alliance with the Americans, spurned the Cassandra in their midst. Nor did Vergennes understand the nature of American politics. He sought to control American foreign policy and during 1781 and 1782 nearly succeeded. But countervailing forces of outlook and character undermined his efforts in Paris and those of his ministers in Philadelphia to manipulate the Americans like so many marionettes on strings.

Certainly, the eight-year war over American independence eroded British power. By the 1783 Treaty of Paris, however, Britain had rid itself of the albatross of administrative and military costs in the colonies, while continuing to enrich itself from trade with the new United States. For many decades thereafter, the Americans would suffer huge trade deficits and remain dependent on superior British manufactured goods, finance, and technology. This dependence at once drained wealth and dynamism from the United States and boosted the prosperity and strength of Britain.

Trade was only one area where America's fate remained entangled with that of Britain and the other great powers. Perhaps the only undisputed clause of the 1783 Treaty of Paris was that Britain recognized American independence. Everything else was open to conditions and interpretations that would keep statesmen, polemicists, demagogues, diplomats, and armed men busy for a couple of generations to come.

With Britain, the most bitter immediate dispute was over just what compensation was due to loyalists and patriots for property confiscated or destroyed during the war. Closely tied to that was exactly how much American debtors owed their British creditors. Then there was the issue of trade. What constraints, if any, should inhibit the ability of Americans and Britons to buy and sell with one another? Would American merchants be restricted from marketing their goods in the British Isles and barred altogether from British colonies in the Caribbean and beyond? The British Army still garrisoned seven forts on American soil. When would those troops withdraw? The British insisted on their "right" to conduct trade and diplomacy with Indian tribes in the United States. Should that be legally recognized? Finally, just where precisely did the American republic end and the British Empire begin?

The 1783 treaty would leave lingering questions of who owned what territory, which would take several generations to resolve fully. That the Mississippi River was America's western boundary seemed clear enough, but no one then knew just where the source of that river was situated and whether it lay in British or American territory. Nor had America's southern boundary been definitively demarcated. Although Britain's treaty with the United States cited the 31st degree latitude, this frontier was undesignated in Britain's treaty with Spain. In the coming decades, the Americans and the Spanish would nearly come to blows over the river and the boundary issues.

The Treaty of Paris may have formally recognized American sovereignty, but the new republic remained grossly dependent on other nations, especially Britain, for money, markets, and manufactured goods. America's leaders dreamed of one day transforming that dependent or subservient relationship into an interdependent or equal relationship with other countries. Yet they understood that for the foreseeable future, they would have to accept these economic and thus strategic vulnerabilities. For now, the United States had to restore commercial relations with Britain and its colonies, while diversifying its commerce with as many other nations as possible. This would allow the United States to enjoy the widest benefits of trade and gradually dilute America's dependence on Britain. Those interests distilled into a simple but powerful maxim—the United States should trade with all, align with none.

But what means were at hand to pursue those ends? The United States was not only virtually powerless but was an oxymoron. The "nation" was a confederation of thirteen sovereign states, each with its own policies, militia, trade, and diplomats. This let foreign powers play the states against one another to reap the best trade and other deals.

Yet these deficits of economic, military, and political power worried few Americans. Most were wildly optimistic when they imagined the coming decades and centuries. They understood that America's greatest strengths were its culture and location on the edge of a sparsely populated continent rich with natural resources. They agreed with Jefferson that the Declaration of Independence perfectly expressed the American mind and that its principles formed the foundation for America's future greatness. John Adams expressed the pervasive belief that "the United States was destined beyond a doubt to be the greatest power on earth, and that within the life of man." To do so meant that the United States would sooner or later break the territorial bounds imposed by the Treaty of Paris and expand across the continent and perhaps the entire Western Hemisphere. Thomas Jefferson envisioned "our confederacy . . . as the nest from which all Americans, North and South, is to be peopled."[28]

Few have captured the essential values of American culture as well as Jean Hector de Crevecoeur, a Frenchman who settled in the United States: "What then is this American, this new man? He is an American, who leaving behind him all his ancient prejudices and manners, receives new ones from the new mode of life he has embraced, the new government he obeys, and the new rank he holds. . . . Here the individuals of all nations are melted into a new race of men, whose labours and posterity will one day cause great changes in the world. . . . The American is a new man, who acts upon new principles; he must therefore entertain new ideas and form new opinions."[29]

That was and remains the ideal. The reality, of course, was and often still is starkly different. Yet from the standpoint of power, what is vital is that most Americans believed that ideal version of themselves and acted on that belief. But those acts were effective only to the extent that they mustered other sources of power to realize them. Otherwise, the belief of Americans in their own greatness was of little practical value.

Given the paucity of hard power in the early republic, America's leaders had to rely on soft power to defend or expand national interests. They continued the strategy that they initiated during the war. The United States would pursue a classic balance-of-power game of advancing national interests by playing other countries off one another. As a weak nation, the United States had to wield diplomatic coquetry to win concessions without yielding anything of substance, especially a commitment to an alliance. John Adams succinctly expressed the foreign policy outlook held by most prominent Americans: "My system is a very simple one: let us preserve the friendships of France, Holland, and Spain, if we can, and in case of war between France and England, let us preserve our neutrality, if possible."[30]

Power was the central theme of George Washington's farewell address to the nation after resigning his command of the army in June 1783. He spoke of America's potential power rooted in its enterprising population, distance from Europe, vast territory filled with natural resources, and vigorous trade. His fear was that his countrymen would squander, rather than develop, those advantages. Independence was only the first step in a long road to national greatness. For Americans, this was "the time of . . . political probation . . . the moment when the eyes of the whole World are turned upon them." The decisions of the present generations would determine whether the United States would "be respectable and prosperous, or contemptible and miserable as a Nation . . . and . . . whether the Revolution must ultimately be considered as a blessing or curse . . . not to the present age alone, for with our fate will the destiny of unborn Millions be involved."[31]

2 0

The Struggle with Britain

I t would be a very cold peace between the United States and Britain. The animosities of most Americans and the outright hatred by some toward Britain would linger for generations. George Washington articulated the pervasive view that Britain remained a clear and present danger to the young republic: "She is at this moment sowing the seeds of jealousy and discontent among the various tribes of Indians on our frontier. . . . And . . . she will improve every opportunity to foment this spirit of turbulence within the bowels of the United States, with a view of distracting our governments, and promoting divisions." Thomas Jefferson was even more outspoken: "In spite of treaties, England is still our enemy. Her hatred is deep-rooted and . . . nothing is wanting with her but the power to wipe us and the land we live on out of existence."[32]

Hard feelings were scarcely confined to Americans. Dominating British politics was a powerful faction still bitter at losing the war and the thirteen colonies. They insisted on a hard-line policy against the people they called ingrates, upstarts, and worse. Very practical strategic and economic reasons grounded these animosities. Despite their nation's overwhelming power, most knowledgeable Britons viewed America with as much trepidation as resentment. If most Americans had a sunny view of their nation's future, for the same reason, Britons looked ahead with dread to a day when American power might well surpass their own.

To forestall that, there was only one sensible policy. Britain had to bottle up the expansion of American territory and economic power. From the end of the War for Independence until the end of the War of 1812, Whitehall pursued a containment policy toward the United States. John Baker Holroyd, Earl Sheffield, was that policy's author. In his 1784 pamphlet "Observations on the Commerce of the American States," he provided a blueprint for keeping the United States weak, disunited, agrarian, and dependent on Britain.

Mercantilism would be the essential component of that containment policy. Americans would be outright prohibited from trading with Britain's colonies and limited in what they could sell in Britain itself. Manufacturers would flood the American market with their high-quality, inexpensive products to reap profits and throttle any efforts by American entrepreneurs to develop their own industries. Shippers would offer cut-rate prices to capture the carrying trade and thus crimp America's merchant fleet. Perennial British trade surpluses would drain coin from the United States. That subsequent scarcity and the high price of capital in the United States would addict Americans to British finance and thus stunt the rise of American capital markets. Meanwhile, British envoys would play off the thirteen states against one another by offering different deals and payoffs. "With prudent management," Sheffield argued, Britain "will have as much of [America's] trade as it will be in her interest to wish for."[33]

Sheffield's proposals formed the foundation for Whitehall's policy toward the United States, which was initiated in 1783. Trade between the two countries was legally restored in April. A decree barred Americans from trading with Britain's West Indian colonies in July. A detailed list of what Americans were permitted to sell in Britain appeared in December. Trade between the United States and the British Isles could be conveyed by vessels of either nation, but only British ships could carry American goods to British colonies.

John Adams had no illusions about the ultimate aim of Whitehall's policies: "Britain has ventured to begin commercial hostilities. I call them hostilities because their direct object is not so much the increase of their own wealth, ships, or sailors, as the diminution of ours."[34] That policy worked—America's dependence on Britain stunted its early economic development and thus its national power.

For a generation or so, the United States would import 90 percent of its manufactured goods from Britain. In contrast, although the United States was Britain's most important foreign market, its trade was much more widespread. From 1778 to 1792, America bought between 10 and 17 percent of Britain's exports. As for British imports, the United States was the second most important source after Russia, but virtually all those goods were raw or semifinished, such as grain and naval stores.[35] As if that were not troubling enough, British bankers and merchants controlled and thus skimmed most of the profits from the trade between the two countries by providing loans, insurance, warehouses, and ships. Finally, as with all other foreign policy issues, there was not one American trade policy toward Britain but thirteen. The British took full advantage of those divisions by playing each state against the others and thus wringing the best deals from all. Thus did American-British trade reflect a classic postcolonial relationship.

The United States could do nothing more than protest that discrimination. The reason was simple. Americans failed to heed a fundamental element of power—there is strength in numbers. About half of the states did try to retaliate against British mercantilism, but their individual efforts actually backfired. Massachusetts, New Hampshire, and Rhode Island forbade British vessels from shipping any goods to or from their ports. The tariffs that British merchants paid to sell in Maryland and North Carolina were four times and in Virginia double those imposed on other foreign merchants. Unfortunately, those efforts only provoked British sneers. British merchants merely diverted their exports to the states with the lowest tariffs and then loaded them on coastal vessels bound for states with higher tariffs. And politicians who imposed high tariffs had to endure the wrath of their own citizens. British goods were less costly, better made, and more diverse that those of any other nation. Then, as now, Americans demanded the best possible deals, no matter how that affected their nation's trade deficit, dependence, and power.[36]

Yet the United States did have a potential ally in fighting against British discrimination. American merchants and state governments were not alone in protesting Britain's policy of barring trade with its colonies. No one hated this prohibition more than West Indian planters. Free trade allowed them the luxury of buying a wider variety of goods at cheaper prices. Without it, they suffered price gouging from the oligopoly of British merchants. In 1783 they tried to get two free trade bills through Parliament, and after that effort failed, they petitioned the government.

Prime Minister William Pitt had originally supported free trade but recanted when pressure from British and Canadian merchants and shipping firms grew too much. He turned over West Indian policy to the newly formed Committee of the Lords of the Privy Council on Trade. The result was predictable. The committee recommended upholding the bar on American trade with Britain's colonies. On August 10, 1784, Privy Council chair Henry Dundas issued an Order in Council to that effect.

The other half of Whitehall's containment policy was aimed at America's territorial ambitions. Theoretically, the 1783 treaty committed the British to accept and respect a United States whose territory spanned those lands between the Atlantic Ocean, the Mississippi River, the Great Lakes, and the 31st parallel. Yet the British spent much of the next three decades doing everything possible to prevent the treaty's fulfillment.

Under the Treaty of Paris, the British were required to evacuate American territory with "all convenient speed." Just what that meant would be up to Whitehall to decide. Evidently, not even a snail's pace was convenient for the British. Although the British would finally leave New York City on December 3, 1783, the Union Jack would fly defiantly above seven frontier forts on American territory for thirteen years after ratification of the 1783 Treaty of Paris.

Whitehall's official policy was that Britain would abandon these forts only after the Americans complied with all of their treaty obligations. The United States violated the treaty by failing to compensate British creditors and loyalists for their losses. Those were not inconsiderable sums. The British government would eventually pay more than 7.5 million pounds sterling to loyalists as compensation for their property losses. By 1783 the debts Americans owed to 194 British creditors amounted to more than 5 million pounds sterling, which included 14 years of accumulated interest.[37]

Whitehall had powerful legal and moral arguments for its positions on debt and compensation. The strategic and economic reasons for lingering in America's Northwest Territory were far more compelling. Each post served both military and economic interests, with Detroit and Michilimackinac the leading regional centers of British trade and influence. The Indians not only supplied furs and bought goods, but they also checked the westward expansion of America's restless and enterprising settler population. The Indian trade in that vast region between the Ohio, Allegheny, and Mississippi Rivers and the Great Lakes would enrich Britain's imperial economy by 40,000 pounds sterling in 1790 alone. Those same Indians, whose trapping and hunting skills were so lucrative to Britain's economic interest in peace, would be invaluable should another war break out with the United States. As they had during America's War for Independence, Indian war parties could once again ravage the American frontier, diverting scarce men, munitions, provisions, and attention from British campaigns elsewhere.

There was a fear factor behind Britain's policy that went far beyond the worry that the expansion of American merchants and settlers across that region would redirect that wealth to themselves. The British frequently justified their occupation with the claim that the Indians would turn on them if they thought the British were abandoning them. Although there was no rational reason to believe that was true, it was nonetheless among those emotionally powerful myths that was widely propagated, believed, and acted on.[38]

During the American war, the British had repeatedly promised the Indians that they would never abandon the Indians to the Americans. Then, with the peace treaty, the British had done just that. In doing so, the British had sacrificed their honor and credibility for peace. How could the tribes or anyone else ever trust Whitehall again?

A few farsighted Americans recognized the danger posed by Britain's contain-ment policy. Tench Coxe dissected that strategy through seven essays of a pam-phlet called "A Brief Inquiry into the Observations of Lord Sheffield." As treasury secretary, Alexander Hamilton carefully studied Whitehall's policies and nurtured ideas that would be the foundation for a set of policies that would eventually help transform America's economy into a manufacturing, financial, commercial, and technological powerhouse and thus break the chains of British containment. At that time, no political leader more fervently tried to counter Britain's strategy than James Madison. His Virginia Port Bill would have shut off that state's mar-kets unless Whitehall opened its colonies to Virginia's exports. British traders eas-ily sidestepped that law, however, by buying from or selling to Virginia through other states. That failure would spur Madison to support a stronger government for the United States.[39]

The growth of American nationalism was the silver lining that George Washington saw in Britain's trade policy: "Their restriction of our trade with them, will facilitate the enlargement of Congressional powers in commercial matters, more than half a century would have otherwise effected."[40] His prediction would be realized with the 1787 Constitution.

Congress did act against the worst British affront to American sovereignty. In 1784 Lt. William Hull was dispatched to Canada to hurry the redcoats on their way. On arriving at Montreal in July, he was stunned to learn from Governor Frederick Haldimand that he had no withdrawal orders. When Hull returned with that message, Congress decided to send an envoy straight to London to settle that and all other lingering conflicts.

The man whom Congress tapped for that mission was among America's most experienced, if not subtle, diplomats. What John Adams lacked in patience or fi-nesse, he made up for with a bulldog persistence in defending American interests. That hardly made him popular with those who sat across the table from him. Yet even someone as affable, witty, and wise as Benjamin Franklin would most likely have experienced as frosty a reception as Adams did when he reached London on May 26, 1785.

Most of the press was hostile to his presence. Although King George III was gra-cious during the audience, thereafter the ministers mostly snubbed Adams and rarely stooped to speak with him about anything of substance. Nor did Whitehall condescend to send a minister to the United States, despite Adams's requests that Britain do so. Everything was calculated to humiliate the envoy from the un-grateful former colonies that had maliciously thrown off Britain's enlightened rule. Adams complained that during his years there, he was subjected to "dry decency and cold civility which appears to have been the premeditated plan from the beginning."[41]

The diplomacy went nowhere. Although, unlike his colleagues, Prime Minister William Pitt was pleasant enough, he made it clear that Britain would retain the western posts until the Americans paid what they owed British merchants and dispossessed loyalists. He would not even discuss the issue of American access to Britain's colonies. Adams would hear that message repeated by all other ministers in the subsequent infrequent and sporadic talks for the next three years until he returned to the United States in February 1788.

Adams failed for a simple reason. America lacked the appropriate hard power for him to wring concessions from Whitehall. Jefferson expressed the general frustration that "to leave her in possession of our posts seems inadmissible, and yet to take them brings on a state of things for which we seem not to be in readiness." He was even pessimistic about wielding the trade card that he periodically advocated: "Perhaps a total suppression of her trade, or an exclusion of her vessels from the carriage of our produce may have some effect, but I believe not greatly. Their passions are too deeply and universally engaged in opposition to us."[42]

21

The Struggle with Spain

Amerca's leaders would be just as frustrated in their efforts to nurture relations and resolve conflicts with Spain as they were with Britain.
Following American independence, Spain's policy swiftly shifted from
aid to containment of the United States.

The roots of that policy lay in the end of the French and Indian War four
decades earlier.[43] Spanish king Charles III received the Louisiana Territory in 1763
as a gift from his cousin, French king Louis XV. Guilt and honor explain Louis's
generosity. His government had enticed Spain in 1761 to belatedly join France in
a war against Britain that had erupted in North America in 1754 and then became
global in 1756, when it spread across much of Europe and the Caribbean and parts
of West Africa, South America, India, East Asia, and the seas linking those distant regions.

Spain's timing in allying with France could not have been worse. France was
bogged down in an unwinnable quagmire in Germany, while Britain had already
conquered Canada. British armadas captured Spain's colonies of Cuba and the
Philippines in 1762. The following year, a thoroughly dispirited Louis and Charles
gave up. Under the Treaty of Paris in 1763, Britain kept Canada from France and
swapped Cuba and the Philippines to Spain in return for East and West Florida. It
was then that Louis tried to assuage his cousin's loss by tossing Louisiana in his lap.

A generation later, Spain again allied with France against Britain. Charles III
did so to avenge his realm's humiliation and loss in 1763 and to weaken an enemy
with whom it had periodically warred for centuries. This time Spain was on the

winning side. In the 1783 Treaty of Paris, Spain kept West Florida, which it had reconquered from Britain, and received East Florida.

Yet victory over Britain cast a dark shadow on the Spanish Empire. Spain was a monarchy and an imperial power, and its rulers viewed America's revolution of liberalism and nationalism with revulsion and fear. Madrid recognized the tremendous risk it had taken in aiding that revolt. What if by helping destroy part of the British Empire, Spain was inadvertently sowing the seeds of liberalism and nationalism that would one day destroy its own empire?

The value of Louisiana and the Floridas to Spain was more prestigious than practical. The costs of ruling and defending those lands far exceeded the revenues they earned the crown. Nearly all of that vast territory was wilderness, broken only by a few clusters of settlements, mostly around Mobile and Pensacola on the Gulf Coast, St. Augustine in northeastern Florida, and from New Orleans to Natchez and Cape Girardeau to St. Louis in the Mississippi Valley. These colonies were an economic backwater of the Spanish Empire. There were no gold or silver mines or industries of any kind. The plantations were relatively small operations. Nearly all the roughly twenty-five thousand subjects were peasants who eked out just enough necessities to survive. The middle class was relatively few in numbers and modest in wealth. The extravagance of the tiny aristocracy may have provoked envy in their lessers but was a pale shadow of what its counterparts enjoyed in Potosi, Mexico City, or Lima.

So just what about those territories could stir pride in a Spaniard? With the gift of Louisiana and the repossession of the Floridas, Spain enjoyed title to nearly all the Americas and the islands in the Western Hemisphere. A map gave the impression that the Caribbean and the Gulf of Mexico were largely Spanish seas. Yet here again, appearances could be deceptive. In reality, Britain's Royal Navy dominated virtually all those waters. Likewise the title to the Louisiana Territory, which included the Mississippi Valley's western watershed (and which in parts extended all the way to the Rocky Mountains a thousand or more miles away), was then much less than it seemed. There were no settlements higher than Natchitoches on the Red River and St. Charles on the Missouri River. A few intrepid Spanish subjects, mostly of French ancestry, did ascend some of those rivers to trade furs from the Indians, but that was the only wealth reaped from that seemingly endless wilderness in the continent's interior.

The only concrete strategic value of Louisiana and the Floridas for Spain was to contain America's restless and enterprising population. The 1783 Treaty of Paris granted the United States title to lands east of the Mississippi River, north of West and East Florida, and south of the Great Lakes. The Spanish, along with the

British, not only were determined that the Americans would never take another inch of land, but hoped to detach and annex the lands and the peoples west of the Appalachian Mountains from the eastern United States.

The key to doing so was the ambiguity over just where the boundary lay between the United States and the Spanish Empire. The British had proclaimed on October 7, 1763, that the boundary between Georgia and Florida was drawn at the St. Mary's River to its source and from there due west to the Apalachicola River, which would divide East from West Florida. West Florida would include all lands bound by the Apalachicola and Mississippi Rivers, the Gulf Coast, and the 31st latitude. When Madrid protested, the British redrew West Florida's boundary northward to the 32nd degree latitude, 30 prime, which stretched between the Mississippi River at the Yazoo River mouth and the Chattahoochee River, which flows into the Apalachicola River, to the east. The assumption was that Spain inherited those declared boundaries when it won the Floridas in 1783. Although Madrid still protested that Florida's northern boundary was much farther north, the British left it at that.

Spain asserted its claim and power in 1784 by announcing the closure of the Mississippi River to American merchants floating flatboats of grain, whiskey, hides, and salted meats to markets in Louisiana and beyond. That, they hoped, would discourage other settlers from migrating west of the Appalachians and would encourage those already there to join the Spanish Empire in return for that market for their goods. Westerners howled in rage, and Congress issued a protest and asked for negotiations. The following year, Madrid dispatched Diego de Gardoqui to be Spain's first minister to the United States. Gardoqui arrived in July 1785 with a mandate to settle the boundary, Mississippi, and trade disputes, but in a way that kept the boundary as far from the 31st degree latitude as possible, denied any navigation right to the Mississippi, and barred any American trade with Spain's colonies. Gardoqui was initially optimistic that he would have no trouble asserting Spanish interests against the Americans. Spain had a strong, if not unassailable, legal case for its claims. The international law of that era did not recognize navigation rights for land-bound states with rivers flowing through other states to the sea. Madrid rejected any notion of being bound by the 31st degree latitude boundary delimitated in the peace between the United States and Britain. Spain's peace with Britain did not demarcate specific boundaries for the Floridas, so the Spanish felt free to draw them as they wished.

Gardoqui had another reason for optimism. He assessed as an easy mark John Jay, who had become the foreign affairs secretary in December 1784. Jay possessed "talent and capacity," but only "enough to cover . . . a weakness" as "a very self-centered man." His other weakness was his wife, Sarah, the daughter of Robert Livingston, the former foreign secretary who was among New Jersey's political and economic elite. Sarah was strikingly beautiful and loved to be the center of attention. "This woman, whom he loves blindly, dominates him and nothing is done without her consent," so "a little management in dealing with her and a few timely gifts will secure the friendship of them both. . . . I believe a skilful hand which knows how to take advantage of favorable opportunities and how to give dinners and above all to entertain with good wine, may profit without appearing to do so."[44]

Gardoqui reckoned that he was just the man for that job. Cuban governor Bernardo de Galvez, his immediate boss, had provided him with three different boundary proposals, each only slightly less outrageous from the point of view of most Americans. The first one cut west across East Florida to the Apalachicola River, then north up the Chattahoochee River until it circled eastward around the headwaters of the Coosa River, then over to the Tennessee River and down it to the Ohio and then the Mississippi. The second would cut westward from the Tennessee River along the present border between Tennessee and Mississippi. The final was the British line, which started at the Yazoo River mouth on the Mississippi across to the Apalachicola River and then down it to the present border of Florida eastward to the Atlantic.

The Spaniard had misjudged his man. Although Gardoqui wined, dined, and even gave gifts to John and Sarah Jay, he never managed to corrupt the secretary of state. During late 1785 until late spring of 1786, they conducted a series of negotiations in which Jay rejected each proposal in turn and insisted on the 31st degree latitude line and navigation of the Mississippi. On May 23 Gardoqui presented Jay with a proposal that included a boundary that angled northwest from East Florida's boundary at the Apalachicola and hit the Mississippi at the Yazoo River mouth. All lands northward to Galvez's first proposed boundary would be an Indian reserve within American territory. As a favor, Spain would pressure the British to withdraw from the posts and allow Americans to trade with Spain but not with its colonies.

Although Jay rejected that proposal as well, Gardoqui's pressure was wearing him down. In August 1786 he asked Congress to revise his instructions so that he could cut a deal with Gardoqui whereby the United States won the 31st degree latitude boundary in return for forbearing the use of, without surrendering the right to navigate, the Mississippi for thirty years. The vote in Congress was seven to five, with the southern states united against the measure. That majority fell short of nine votes necessary for approval.[45]

That rejection theoretically empowered Jay at the negotiating table. Yet the best he could wring from Gardoqui was to submit the boundary to a joint commission, to grant most-favored-nation status, to eliminate the Indian barrier, and to limit the treaty to ten years, with either side able to withdraw on six months' notice. That treaty would die stillborn. When Jay presented the proposed treaty, Congress exploded in debate mostly over what Jay had given up. The final vote was that same seven to five split between northern and southern states. The treaty died because the vote was two states short of the nine needed for ratification.

Then, as now, Westerners reacted with either rage or relief to government policies back east. A crisis erupted as word spread among them that a majority of states were willing to sacrifice the Westerners' "right" to navigate the Mississippi River to the sea. Enraged frontiersmen spoke of breaking away as an independent nation or joining Britain or even Spain.

Throughout American history, there have been citizens who have betrayed their country, a country they nearly always claimed to have loved. Greed, often leavened by a desire for vengeance and a love of intrigue, has been the key motive. James Wilkinson is among the most notorious of American traitors.[46] He was a war veteran but renowned more for his prowess at political intrigue than in battle. In 1784 he settled in Kentucky and quickly rose to prominence as a merchant, a land speculator, and a politician. Although his political popularity rested mostly on his vociferous demands for Kentucky statehood, he secretly desired a far different fate for that region and people. In April 1787 he and his men packed a flatboat with tobacco, hams, and corn and began that long float and pole down to New Orleans. In a July 2 meeting with Governor Esteban Miro and Intendant Martin de Navarro, Wilkinson promised to detach Kentucky and join it to Spain in return for payments in cash, land, and trade monopolies. Miro and Navarro eagerly accepted his formal pledge of allegiance to Spain and gave "Agent Thirteen" the first of numerous payments for his intrigues.

After returning to the United States, Wilkinson began weaving a web of conspirators that would eventually include such prominent public figures as John Brown, Harry Innes, Benjamin Sebastian, and, most notorious of all, Aaron Burr. Over the years, many other Westerners would associate briefly with the Wilkinson cabal, talk directly with Spanish agents, or advocate a sovereign trans-Appalachian state, including such prominent leaders as Andrew Jackson, George Rogers Clark, John Sevier, James Robertson, and William Blount.

Not only were Easterners well aware of the prevailing western rage, but they had heard the rumors of conspiracy and outright treason and feared the potentially disastrous consequences for American power. George Washington, for one, perceived that "the western settlers . . . stand as it were upon a pivot; the touch of a feather would turn them any way."[47]

Yet the uproar among Westerners, if not the treason of those like Wilkinson, simmered down after they learned that Congress had rejected Jay's treaty and that the new king, Charles IV, had decreed in December 1788 that henceforth Americans could navigate the Mississippi through Spanish territory and sell goods in New Orleans and other towns after paying average tariffs of 15 percent. The king also opened his empire to immigrants as long as they swore allegiance to Spain and converted to Catholicism.

That put American relations with Spain on the back burner for the next half-dozen years. Even during the height of negotiations between Jay and Gardoqui, most Americans were far less concerned about the conflicts with Spain than about those with Britain. They believed that sooner or later, the Spanish territories would fall into the nation's hands like ripe fruit from a tree. This belief stemmed from four related forces: the scarcity of Spain's settlers and troops in those territories; the ever-swelling American population westward into American and Spanish lands; America's distance from Spain; and the nearly incessant European conflicts that distracted and bogged down the great powers.[48]

Thomas Jefferson was a leading exponent of this view and followed the events beyond the Appalachians with keen interest. While he sympathized with the plight of the western settlers, he wanted them to remain in the United States. To his friend John Brown, who was, unbeknownst to him, part of Wilkinson's cabal, he offered the sensible advice that "the Western Country . . . defer pushing their right to that navigation to extremity as long as they can do without it tolerably. . . . A time of peace will not be the surest for obtaining this object. Those therefore who have influence in the new country would act wisely to endeavor to keep things quiet until the western parts of Europe shall be engaged in war."[49] For now, patience was the best policy: "We should take care . . . not to think it for the interest of that great continent to press too soon on the Spaniards. Those countries cannot be in better hands." If Spain posed a threat to the United States, it was from weakness, rather than strength. The great fear was that the Spanish were "too feeble to hold them till our population can be sufficiently advanced to gain it from them piece by piece. The navigation of the Mississippi we must have."[50]

22

The Struggle with France

France was among the great powers dedicated to containing America economically, territorially, and militarily. Versailles "sought to keep the United States friendly but weak" while nurturing bilateral trade that weaned America from dependence on Britain.[51] The 1778 trade and alliance treaties formed the legal foundation of the relationship between France and the United States. Vergennes insisted on a strict adherence to the letter of those treaties, especially the clause that made the United States and France eternal allies.

American policy toward France was simple enough—the Americans sought to expand trade and end the alliance. As for trade, the government did not have to do anything—American exports to and imports from France rose steadily after the war. The stickler in the relationship was the clause in the alliance treaty forever binding the two nations. The Americans insisted that the Treaty of Paris ended the alliance. To lend weight to that claim, they accused the French of having seriously violated the spirit of their original alliance for having tried to trump American with Spanish interests on the Mississippi River navigation and southern boundary issues; indeed, Versailles had conspired with Madrid to contain the United States east of the Appalachian Mountains. Nor did French intrigues end there. The Americans would later learn that during the peace negotiations, the French had talked with the British of breaking up the colonies into an independent New England and subservient middle and southern regions and had toyed with the notion of a peace based on *uti possedetis*, which would have allowed the British to keep New York City, Charleston, Savannah, and their surrounding regions.

Benjamin Franklin remained America's minister to France. Although he dutifully conveyed the mind of Congress to Vergennes, in July 1784 he signed with the foreign minister a consular convention that would heighten, rather than diminish, American suspicions toward France. The convention essentially rejected any notion that the United States was a sovereign state. Diplomats accused of crimes would be judged by a consular court of that mission, rather than by the criminal or civil courts of the host country. To American nationalists, the worst tenet let the French conduct separate diplomatic relations with each state, thus allowing them to play each against the others. Yet given the jealousy with which each state then guarded its sovereignty, that convention was perhaps the best that Franklin could do. Nonetheless, Secretary of State John Jay was horrified when he received the convention. He convinced Congress not to ratify it but to return it to Paris for renegotiation.

That convention was Franklin's last diplomatic effort and was hardly a triumph. Ill health forced him to give up his post and return to the United States later in 1784. As the quintessential progressive American—learned, inventive, witty, curious, open-minded, generous, practical, hardworking, and easygoing—he left behind a reserve of goodwill toward the United States that has endured through today, although at times it has been strained on occasion as interests clashed between the two nations.

Thomas Jefferson was appointed the new minister to France. On arriving in 1784, he famously remarked that Benjamin Franklin could never be replaced, only followed.[52] Jefferson proved to be an able diplomat in his own right. For very practical reasons, he saw public relations as his mission's central role: "It is very much in our interest to keep up the affection of this country for us, which is considerable. The court has no affections, but those of the people whom they govern influence their decisions even in the most arbitrary governments."[53]

All along Jefferson firmly upheld the position that America's duties to France ended with the Treaty of Paris. That assertion was more rooted in sentiment than in law. The wording of the 1778 alliance treaty was certainly ambiguous but seemed to entangle America and France in an open-ended commitment to each other.

Jefferson's most notable diplomatic achievement was to negotiate a more favorable consular convention than the one Franklin sent back to the United States in 1784. Under the 1788 convention, France recognized "the United States of America" as a sovereign state; the agreement would last twelve years. Yet the convention still bore that troubling extraterritorial tenet, which let a diplomatic mission, rather than the host nation's courts, deal with any envoy accused of crimes.

Meanwhile, in Philadelphia, Eleonor Francois Elie, the comte de Moustier, remained France's minister to the United States. He was perhaps not the best choice to serve in that post because he ill-concealed his contempt for American manners, cooking, and society. His feelings were stronger than his intellect, and thus he could not restrain his natural tendency toward vanity, pomp, and arrogance. In all, he alienated far more of America's national elite than he charmed.

Congress assigned John Jay the task of seeking Moustier's recall. In October 1788 Jay passed that mission on to Jefferson in Paris. Jefferson dutifully brought the request to Foreign Minister Armand Marc, the comte de Montmorin de Saint-Herem, who had replaced Vergennes the previous year. It took until October 1789 before Moustier would actually leave the United States. It would be another year after that before Paris got around to filling that post. During that time, the charge d'affaires, Louis-Guillaume Otto, handled the mission.[54] The delay was largely due to the convulsions racking France after the revolution erupted in May 1789.

23

The Struggle with the Tribes

U nder the 1783 Treaty of Paris, Britain conceded to the United States an enormous amount of territory, with the western lands nearly twice the size of those already settled along the eastern seaboard. Countless pioneers, merchants, and land speculators, along with Congress and seven states, were eager to exploit that vast landscape as soon as possible. Two obstacles would delay and distort that process.

The first was the conflict between Congress and those seven states over who owned what of the western lands. Citing their colonial charters, Massachusetts, Connecticut, New York, Virginia, North Carolina, South Carolina, and Georgia asserted the right to broad swaths of western lands, with some stretching as far as the Pacific Ocean. The six states without claims preferred that Congress, rather than their rivals, take title.

Congress itself was desperate to control the West. During the war, with no power to tax and only so much money to be raised by tariffs, a bankrupt Congress could merely promise soldiers land in proportion to their rank in return for their continued service. And even with the war over, Congress could pay only part of its expenses with tariff receipts. Only by selling land could Congress pay its budget and service its debt.

That standoff cracked in February 1780, when New York promised to cede its claim to Congress if all other states would follow suit. In September 1780 Congress called on the holdouts to give up their claims. One by one, the others did so—Virginia in 1784, Massachusetts in 1785, Connecticut in 1786, South Carolina in 1787, North Carolina in 1790, and Georgia in 1802.

That pace was too glacial for Congress. On March 1, 1784, Congress declared that it held undisputed title to the territory and would henceforth act accordingly. The debate within Congress then shifted from who owned the land to what to do with it. The question of how to divvy it up among veterans had already been resolved, but what about everyone else who wanted land? Was it better for Congress to sell land in small allotments to aspiring homesteaders or in large blocs to speculators who would in turn dispose of it as they saw fit?

Congress opted for the quick disposal method. Under the 1785 Land Ordinance, the land would first be surveyed, then divided into six-square-mile townships composed of 640-acre lots going for $640 each. With that policy, however, Congress sold little land and made little money. Speculators with bags of worthless script would have been happy to pay for those lots and then sell them off if they could have received something more valuable in return. Then there was the problem of settlers already occupying that land. When a landlord appeared at their doorstep with a title and a demand for payment, a common response was a raised rifle and an order to leave.

Congress then split the western land into two vast realms governed by different laws. The 1787 Northwest Ordinance affected all those lands north of the Ohio River. That territory would eventually be carved up among three to five states, depending on the settlement patterns. The process would unfold in three stages. At first the president would appoint a governor and three judges to administer the territory. When more than five thousand males settled a region, they could form an assembly and elect a nonvoting delegate to Congress. Finally, when the people in a region surpassed sixty thousand, they could write a constitution and form a state. All settlers were guaranteed the rights of freedom of speech, assembly, religion, habeas corpus, trial by jury, and security of contract. A man could vote if he owned at least fifty acres, and he could run for office with at least two hundred acres. Each township was required to have a public school, to be financed by land sales. Slavery was forbidden. Finally, the law guaranteed "good faith" with the Indians. The 1790 Southwest Ordinance, which governed the territory south of the Ohio River, was nearly identical but for one crucial tenet—slavery was allowed.

Forging a consensus among the states over who owned the western lands and then what to do with this territory had been tough enough. Yet far more daunting was what to do about the estimated fifty thousand Indians scattered in clusters of villages across those lands. The United States would not officially recognize the Indian tribes as "domestic dependent nations" until 1831 but treated them as subjects from the beginning of the war in 1775. Any armed resistance was considered a rebellion that must be crushed and the survivors punished with territorial losses. Any aid by outside powers to the Indians was considered interference in the internal affairs of the United States and thus an act of aggression.

With each tribe, the Americans sought to designate a chief empowered to make legally binding treaties on behalf of his people. The problem was that no tribe had such a chief. Indeed, the notion of tribe itself was largely a fiction. A "tribe" might consist of a dozen or so villages that shared a dialect and a tradition of association in marriage, trade, diplomacy, and war.

The primary identity and loyalty of Indians was to their village. Yet even then diversity, rather than unity, was the norm. Each village was split among numerous clans, societies, and political factions. In most villages, decisions were reached by consensus among the elders, although any interested men and, in some places, women could voice their views during the council. Although nearly every village had a "chief" or a headman, he was merely the first among equals and empowered to persuade, rather than command. Chiefs were recognized for their skill in forging accord among all those entitled with a say on controversial issues that protected the village while salving the feelings of those with different views.

No issue was more divisive than whether or not to go to war. While most younger men longed to win glory on the warpath, most elders feared that war would bring death and devastation to the village. Ideally, the warriors would carry back not merely scalps and other loot, but also captives to replenish the people. A couple of centuries of warfare with Europeans (as well as peaceful cohabitation) had lightened the skin tones of native peoples as countless whites were assimilated. But what if those warriors who were killed exceeded in number the captives who were eventually integrated into the village? This was no small concern. Wars and epidemics rendered the populations of villages and tribes in continuous flux. Populations were devastated and then slowly recovered. Depleted villages amalgamated or uprooted themselves and sought refuge farther from their enemies.

Although divisions among and within villages appeared to be endless, nearly all Indians shared an interest—to keep American hunters and settlers as far from their lands as possible. They also shared a vulnerability—they had grown dependent on muskets and munitions with which to hunt and war, along with having a fondness for an array of other goods that only whites could make, such as iron pots, glass beads, calico shirts and skirts, silver ornaments, vivid paints, and alcohol, to name the more prominent. These items could be obtained only through trade in times of peace and as gifts from a white ally or by plunder from an enemy in times of war.

Indian diplomacy was no different than in any other region of the world inhabited by peoples with conflicting interests. Faced with an outside threat, Indians followed the principles of "divide and conquer" and "the enemy of my enemy is my friend." Against the overwhelming American threat, Indians sought aid from the British and Spanish empires. The British and the Spanish, in turn, were just as eager to enlist Indian allies in their respective containment policies against the United States.

In early America there were endless conflicts between where lines were drawn on maps and where people actually lived or wanted to live. The frontier was both a magnet and a refuge for Americans who wanted more than they could get from their lives back east. After the Independence War, many were veterans whom Congress had promised land for their service. Many were escaping debt, scandal, and spite. Virtually all believed that they could carve a better life from the wilderness. That desire often conflicted with the native peoples living on those lands.

Settlers first ventured into the territory that became Kentucky and Tennessee during America's War for Independence. With peace, that trickle of people became a flood. In a half-dozen years from the war's end until the 1790 census, the populations of Kentucky and Tennessee soared from fewer than several thousand and several hundred to 73,677 and 35,691, respectively.

That human tide brutally shoved aside the native peoples and severed the trade and war paths that once crossed those lands. The tribes now were split between the northwest and the southwest regions of lands that were claimed and increasingly occupied by the Americans. For aid, the northwest Indians mostly looked to the British forts in the Great Lakes, as well as to the handful of French settlements now under Spanish rule on the west side of the upper Mississippi River. The southwest tribes had to rely on the Spanish, who controlled the Floridas and lands west of the Mississippi River.

That horde of settlers would eventually provoke war with the northwest Indians. People who came to Kentucky later often discovered that the best lands were already taken by those who got there earlier. Ever more land-hungry settlers crossed the Ohio River to its north bank and began clearing the forest.

At that time, the northwest tribes that would be directly involved in diplomacy and war with the United States for the next three decades included the Shawnee, who were mostly clustered in western Ohio; the Miami and related people, such as the Wea and Kickapoo, in three clumps of villages on the upper Wabash River; the Potawatomi in northwestern Indiana; and the Wyandot and the Delaware in northwestern Ohio.

A majority in Congress was sincerely interested in forging peaceful and just relations between the United States and the tribes. In 1785 Fort Harmar was established where the Muskingham River flows into the Ohio River. Lt. Col. Josiah Harmar, then the highest-ranking officer in the roughly six-hundred-man "army," commanded the scattered infantry companies that somehow were supposed to keep peace between the Indians and the Americans. In 1786 Congress established northern and southern Indian departments, split by the Ohio River and each headed by a superintendent. The 1787 Northwest Ordinance pledged the "utmost good faith shall always be observed toward the Indians, their lands and property shall not be taken from them without consent; and in their property, rights and liberty, they shall never be invaded or disturbed, unless in just and lawful wars authorized by Congress." Congress appointed Arthur St. Clair the governor of the Northwest Territory.

Yet the goal of good relations conflicted with the need of Congress to sell lands for revenues and the demands of powerful land companies to open more territory for settlement. To that end, Congress dispatched diplomats who negotiated three treaties, which took more land from the northern Indians. Under the Treaty of Fort Stanwix, signed on October 22, 1784, the Iroquois ceded nearly all their land in northern Pennsylvania and southern New York. Under the Treaty of Fort McIntosh of January 21, 1785, a group of mostly Delaware and Wyandot chiefs ceded most of Ohio east of the Great Miami River. Under the Treaty of Fort Finney of January 31, 1786, a council of mostly Shawnees confirmed that cession. The United States bought those treaties with the usual piles of trade goods and annual payments in kind.

Each of these treaties was fatally flawed. None had been ratified by the tribal councils. Indeed, Indians who had not attended the peace talks condemned those who did for succumbing to the bribes, the alcohol, and the empty promises by whites. Yet the American government and settlers would act on the assumption that all three treaties were legally binding.

Tribal leaders sent repeated warnings to the United States government that squatters must go away or else. Warriors took matters into their own hands and attacked isolated farms and hamlets. In 1786 Kentuckians launched two retaliatory raids against Indians north of the Ohio, that of George Rogers Clark against the Miami Indians who were threatening Vincennes and that of Benjamin Logan against the Shawnee town of Mackanack. The Kentuckians provoked ever more warriors of those and other villages to hostilities.

Despite the swelling danger, a group of settlers founded the town of Marietta across the Muskingham River from Fort Harmar in April 1788. Governor St. Clair took up residence at Marietta in July. Within weeks the Indians launched the first of numerous raids against that settlement. St. Clair sent runners to the tribes calling for a peace council. Eventually, twenty-seven chiefs and several hundred warriors appeared in late December 1788 for several weeks of talks and feasts. Under the Treaty of Fort Harmar, signed on January 9, 1789, the Ohio tribes ceded the land east of the Muskingham River to the United States. That peace would not last much longer than it took the ink to dry on the document.

The situation was nearly as explosive among the southwest Indians. The main tribes there included the Lower Creeks and the Upper Creeks across much of Alabama and western Georgia, the Chickasaw in western Tennessee and northern Mississippi, the Choctaw in central and southern Mississippi, and the Cherokee across western North Carolina, northern Georgia, and southeastern Tennessee.

As in the northwest, the diplomacy was triangular, rather than bilateral. The Indians of the "Old Southwest" played off the Americans and the Spanish as skillfully as their "Old Northwest" brethren played the Americans and the British. The Spanish, like the British, sought to rally as many villages and tribes as possible into a vast buffer state that could contain the United States. They conducted trade and diplomacy at Mobile and Pensacola with the Creeks, in Natchez with the Choctaw, and in San Fernando (modern Memphis) with the Chickasaw. The Spanish wrote off diplomacy and trade with the Cherokees as being too remote to bother.

The Creek confederacy was the most powerful of the southwest tribes and the most firm in resisting the Americans. No Creek leader was more prominent than Alexander McGillivray, the son of a Creek mother and a Georgian trader. In 1784 he scored an astonishing diplomatic coup when he united the Creeks with the Chickasaws and the Choctaws in negotiating a treaty with Louisiana's governor, Esteban Miro, whereby Spain would protect those tribes and not allow any Americans into their territory without a passport. To supply the southwest Indians, the Spanish granted a license to the Englishmen William Panton and Robert Leslie, who in turn formed a partnership with McGillivray. With their headquarters at Pensacola, the company of Panton and Leslie reaped huge profits from a network of traders across the region.

Each of those tribes was threatened by Americans from different states coming from different directions. The Cherokee and the Creeks faced the most pressure from American expansion and over the decades had fought numerous wars in a futile struggle to hold back that tide. Georgia was the most aggressive of the states against those tribes. Then there were the land companies. During the late 1780s and into the 1790s, companies from South Carolina, Georgia, and North Carolina schemed to claim and settle land that the state of Georgia had fraudulently sold them in the Yazoo River Valley.

Determined to avoid a war, Congress sent peace commissioners among the southwestern tribes in 1785, but both Georgia and McGillivray prevented them from reaching the Creeks. Ever more skirmishes flared between the Georgians and the Creeks along their long frontier. The nightmare fear in Congress was that the United States might end up fighting simultaneous wars with both the northwest and the southwest Indians, wars that the new nation could not afford and might not win.

24

The Struggle with the Barbary States

A merica's involvement in the Arab world is not recent but goes back to the first years of the early republic. Relations were troubled from the start. The Barbary states of Morocco, Algiers, Tunis, and Tripoli stretched from west to east across North Africa before reaching Egypt. Those four states shared several vital characteristics. They were all predominantly Arab and Muslim and had essentially broken free from the Ottoman Empire ruled from Constantinople. They also earned most of their income by demanding protection money from other states. The consequences of not paying up were severe—merchant vessels and cargoes of recalcitrant states were confiscated and the crews sold into slavery.

The European states, great and small alike, deemed it wiser to pay than fight the Barbary states. They viewed the shakedowns as simply a business expense, albeit a steep one. Ransoming crews was more expensive than handing over tribute up front, while the costs of fighting wars with the Barbary states could be tenfold or more. Meanwhile, the profits from trading directly with these states or elsewhere within the Mediterranean basin were so lucrative that the fees seemed paltry in comparison.

During America's colonial era, Whitehall paid annual tribute to each of the Barbary states so that the vessels of the British Empire could sail unmolested through the Mediterranean Sea and the adjacent Atlantic Ocean. With independence, that protective umbrella vanished. Thus began the new nation's problems with the Barbary states.

For reasons of both penury and pride, the Americans refused to pay up. Indeed, the confederation was so strapped for cash that it could not even afford to send envoys to those states. Instead, the Americans asked first the French and then other countries that recognized their independence to intercede on their behalf.

That effort bore some good. In 1778 Sidi Mohamet, Morocco's ruler, forbade the corsairs of his realm from attacking the Americans but requested a treaty of commerce and friendship with the United States. Although Congress signaled its gratitude and willingness to negotiate a treaty, years passed, and the opportunity was buried deeper beneath other priorities and memories. Tired of waiting, Sidi Mohamet ordered his corsairs to seize an American ship, the *Betsy*, in October 1783.

That got Congress's attention. The *Betsy* was released through Spain's good offices and a promise that the United States would soon open negotiations. In 1785 Congress appointed Thomas Barclay its envoy and appropriated $20,000 for the payoffs necessary to fulfill his mission. Barclay did not arrive in Morocco until June 1786 but swiftly negotiated a treaty by which Americans were allowed to sail unmolested and trade freely with Morocco after making a "gift" of $10,000; there would be no annual tribute.

The hope was that the treaty with Morocco's emperor would be a model for deals with the other Barbary states. To that end, Congress appropriated $80,000 to be split among Algiers, Tunis, and Tripoli, whose respective rulers were titled dey, bey, and bashaw. For those other states, however, it was business as usual. They demanded fees that the Americans believed were exorbitant and, when Congress did not pay up, authorized their corsairs to confiscate American ships, cargoes, and crews. On declaring war against the United States, the Algerians captured two vessels and held their crews for ransom. Congress dispatched John Lamb to Algiers to try to free the captives. The dey initially demanded $200,000 for the twenty-two prisoners but eventually lowered the price to $59,496.

Meanwhile, in Paris, John Adams negotiated with Tripoli's envoy, Abdrahaman, for a treaty. Once again, the fee demanded was too steep for the United States. In their encounters, Adams was as fascinated as he was frustrated by Abdrahaman and could not determine whether he was "a consummate politician in art and address, or . . . a benevolent and wise man."[55]

Word of the huge bribes demanded by the Barbary states provoked loud, indignant demands for war by some in Congress and beyond. Rather than go it alone, some advocated that the United States form an alliance among aggrieved countries to fight the Barbary states. From Paris, however, both John Adams and his successor, Thomas Jefferson, advised Congress that it was wiser to pay than fight the Barbary states.[56] Yet Congress lacked the money even to do that. The result was a diplomatic stalemate that would stretch for more than a half-dozen years, during which the Americans lost only two vessels, their cargoes, and twenty-one captives left to rot and die in an Algiers dungeon.

25

"A More Perfect Union"

In all its struggles with foreign and native peoples, the United States lacked virtually every essential ingredient of power, the most glaring of which was unity. Lord Grenville expressed the prevailing foreign view: "We do not know whether they are under one head, directed by many, or whether they have any head at all."[57] On more issues than not, Congress gridlocked, rather than agreed. And in those relatively rare instances when a delicate consensus was hammered out, one or more maverick states could wreck it by going their own way. The British, the French, and the Spanish took full advantage of those divisions by playing the states off one another and Congress. The nation's problems hardly ended there. The confederation and the states were all deeply in debt; the currency was worthless; inflation was rife; the economy was depressed; and lawlessness was spreading.

George Washington was among ever more Americans who despaired at the confederation's weakness. In June 1783 he warned Congress that without a strong central government, "we shall be left nearly in a state of nature, or . . . progression from the extreme of anarchy to the extreme of tyranny, that arbitrary power is most easily established on the ruins of liberty abused to licentiousness." To James Madison, Washington insisted that Congress make a crucial choice: "We are either a United people, or we are not. If the former, let us, in all matters of general concern act as a nation, which have national objects to promote and a National character to support—If we are not, let us no longer act a farce by pretending to it."[58] No one worked more tirelessly for a national government than Alexander Hamilton. Under the pseudonym "The Continentalist," he wrote a series of essays in 1782 and 1783 that called for transforming the confederation into a federation through a constitutional convention. In Congress, however, devotees of state sovereignty checkmated each resolution that took up Hamilton's proposal.

An opening occurred in 1784 when a boundary dispute erupted between Virginia and Maryland. Congressman James Madison proposed settling the conflict through arbitration, with each state making its case before a panel of judges from other states. The commission convened at Washington's Mt. Vernon plantation on March 25, 1785. After quickly resolving that dispute, those present began discussing the array of problems facing the United States. Madison once again led by proposing that those problems be systematically addressed by delegates from each state meeting at Annapolis in September 1786. The urgency to act was spurred by a rebellion against taxes and for debt relief, which erupted in western Massachusetts in 1785 led by John Shay. Although within a few months the state crushed that revolt, the fear was that similar rebellions would erupt in other places that had suffered similar harsh and worsening economic conditions.

The Annapolis meeting lasted only three days before the eight states that sent delegates reached a consensus—a convention should be convened of all of the states to deal with all of the challenges facing the nation. Hamilton wrote the report summarizing the issues raised at the Annapolis meeting and petitioning Congress to authorize such a convention. Congress did so on February 21, 1787.

Although delegates had been gathering for weeks and the convention ceremonially opened at Independence Hall in Philadelphia on May 14, the work did not officially begin until May 29, when a quorum of delegates from seven states was present. During the next four months, fifty-five delegates from twelve states would voice their hopes, fears, and suggestions. Only Rhode Island refused to participate. Nearly all of those who attended favored a stronger government but differed widely on just what was appropriate. Various proposals were aired, debated, and deconstructed.[59]

In devising a government, the framers valued the hard school of the real world over lofty idealism. Two experiences guided their work. One was the utter failure of the existing political system, the confederation of thirteen sovereign states. The other was the success of the states in creating their own respective republics. The former taught them clearly what not to do and the latter what they possibly could do. These lessons were all about power.

Power was the central concern when the framers crafted the Constitution. They wanted a system that at once mobilized and contained power. They knew well two extreme models not to follow. To them, Britain's constitutional monarchy and their own confederation, respectively, personified the Scylla of tyranny and Charybdis of near anarchy.

What the delegates created was succinctly expressed by Benjamin Franklin as he strolled out of Independence Hall after joining his colleagues in signing the Constitution on September 17, 1787. A woman from the crowd anxiously asked him the nature of the government they had created. To that, he smiled and replied, "A republic, madam, if you can keep it."[60]

Those versed in political philosophy but not privy to the convention's deliberations would be surprised by the type of republic the Founders had devised. A classic republic was small in population, territory, and ambition. Political theorists, most notably Charles Louis de Secondat, Baron Montesquieu, and David Hume, had warned that only small republics could possibly retain their institutions and virtues. They pointed to the Roman Republic, which, as it expanded into an empire, was transformed into a tyranny. The lesson was that republicanism and imperialism did not mix. As Hume put it, "Extensive conquests, when pursued, must be the ruin of every free government."[61] Yet although a small republic might better contain internal dangers, it was vulnerable to the aggression of more powerful states.

The winning argument at the convention was that a modern republic could be any size, although bigger was actually better. Not only was there was no trade-off between liberties and security, they reinforced each other. The greater America's territory and population, the stronger it would be to resist both domestic and foreign enemies.

Those who advocated a modern republic had a realistic view of human nature. People were a mélange of mostly good, along with less laudable characteristics, but generally were driven by self-interest, rather than by virtue. That, however, was not an insurmountable barrier to realizing a republic. Indeed, the self-interest of individuals and groups could actually serve the public interest if they were properly handled.

The key was to encourage the diversification of interest groups, with all struggling against all and thus preventing any one or a small coterie from reigning supreme. To that end, power was deliberately diffused and overlapped among the national, state, and local governments; the executive, legislative, and judicial branches; the Senate and the House of Representatives; and the government and the people. In each of those four areas, the framers carefully divvied up and overlapped the duties and the powers of government to promote both struggle and cooperation.

The Constitution's preamble clearly expresses the government's ultimate source of power, along with its duties. "We the People of the United States" establish a government dedicated to "a more perfect union," justice, domestic tranquility, common defense, the general welfare, "and the blessings of liberty to ourselves and our posterity." The "supremacy clause" makes the Constitution the "law of the land," bolstered by any amendments, national laws, and international treaties that do not violate its principles. The "enabling clause" empowered Congress and the president to enact all laws "necessary and proper" to fulfilling the Constitution.

The framers understood that, as Hamilton put it, "the vigor of government is essential to the security of liberty" and for the United States to survive, let alone thrive, in an international system beset by persistent threats and fleeting opportunities. On international issues, a powerful executive would work together with an equally powerful legislature, with their different strengths reinforcing each other. The executive would exemplify "decision, activity, secrecy, and dispatch," while the legislature would be composed of "a chosen body of citizens . . . whose wisdom may best discern the true interest of the country, and whose patriotism and love of justice will be least likely to sacrifice it to temporary or partial considerations."[62]

Hamilton was especially concerned to create institutions that could resist a rush to war. The study of history revealed that "momentary passion and immediate interests have a more active and imperious control over human conduct than general or remote considerations."[63] Madison was just as fearful of that possibility. He reminded Americans of the "universal truth that the loss of liberty at home is to be charged to provisions against danger, real or pretended, from abroad."[64] Here again, the solution was to divide power to force the executive and the legislative branches to work together. Congress was empowered to declare, fund, and oversee war, while the president was ultimately in charge. For national defense, the Constitution specifically authorized the creation of an army and a navy and the authority to regulate and mobilize the militia.

The Constitution was more a sketch than a blueprint for the new government. Although the framers sought to make the Constitution's principles crystal clear, they intentionally left some parts vague. An inability to agree or inattention to detail at times explained those ambiguities. Most important, however, the framers wanted to devise a constitution that future generations could adapt to their own needs and desires.

The Constitution that emerged after more than four months of debate during that long, sweltering summer of 1787 finessed a conundrum of power: too much concentrated in too few hands would lead to tyranny; too little dispersed across too many hands would lead to gridlock and even anarchy. Through a series of compromises, the framers found and institutionalized a golden mean of power between those extremes.

The key question about power that they answered was, who has the right to rule? During their revolution, Americans won sovereignty twice, first from Britain and then from the states. The Constitution's framers succeeded in rooting sovereignty in "We, the people" while making the federal government the highest ultimate expression of that authority. Thus was the United States transformed from a committee presiding over a confederation of states into a government ruling a nation.

The Constitution would be implemented only if nine states ratified it. That would prove to be a tough battle. The Constitution provoked rage among those who fervently believed that the states were sovereign. Others believed that the Constitution did not go far enough and demanded that it be amended with a list of rights.

Alexander Hamilton was the Constitution's most fervent and prolific advocate. He asked James Madison and John Jay to join him in writing a series of essays that explained and justified the Constitution. The result, known as the Federalist Papers, is the world's greatest treatise on liberal political philosophy. Of the eighty-five essays that appeared between October 27, 1787, and April 4, 1788, Hamilton penned fifty-one, Madison twenty-nine, and Jay five. The theme of the Federalist Papers was the vital necessity of a strong republic to protect liberties, develop the economy, and defend the nation from foreign threats. Although the essays appeared in the *Independent Journal* in New York City, they were quickly copied and spread across the United States.

Those who condemned the Constitution, known as the anti-Federalists, launched their own barrage of essays demanding that the states reject ratification. They were enraged that the Constitution vested sovereignty in "the people," rather than in "the states." But none of the anti-Federalist tracts could match the eloquence, profundity, and reason of the Federalists'.

Starting with Delaware on December 7, 1787, one state after another ratified the Constitution. The Constitution took effect on July 26, 1788, when New York became the ninth state to vote in favor of ratification.

Americans finally had a truly national government. The question thereafter has been just what they would do with it.

Consequences
What Did It All Mean?

The American Revolution unfolded through two phases: winning independence and creating "a more perfect union."

Hot lead and cold steel determined American independence. The Americans lost more battles than they won, but their ability to stay in the fight, replenish their ranks, repeatedly square off with the redcoats and the Hessians, and capture enemy armies at Saratoga and Yorktown finally shattered the resolve of the king and Parliament. Yet the Americans could not have won independence without massive French military and financial aid.

Although the French began feeding the American rebels money, muskets, munitions, and other essential instruments of war within a year after the fighting broke out, they would have never dared to openly ally with the United States against Britain had not an American army captured General Burgoyne, along with fifty-five hundred British and Hessian troops, at Saratoga in October 1777. And even then Versailles might not have taken the plunge without the deft diplomacy of Benjamin Franklin and his colleagues in Paris. But Saratoga itself would have been impossible had not George Washington and his army not only repeatedly evaded destruction by superior enemy forces, but captured or killed more than a thousand Hessians at Trenton in December 1776 and trounced British soldiers at Princeton in January 1777. With an army of American and French troops, Washington was able to corner and force General Cornwallis to surrender his seventy-five hundred troops at Yorktown in October 1781. After that, Whitehall's bitter acceptance of American independence was only a matter of time.

Military battles were relatively infrequent during the leisurely pace of eighteenth-century warfare. Political battles, however, were incessant. Within and beyond Congress, those who championed liberty argued over just how to pull it off. With independence, most patriots had barely caught their breath when the barrages of hot words erupted again, this time over whether the United States would be thirteen independent states or one sovereign nation and, if the latter, under what form of government. That debate peaked during the sweltering, seeming endless months in Philadelphia from May to September 1787, when delegates hammered out the Constitution.

Although with the Constitution's ratification, the revolution came to a symbolic and substantive end, ever since then Americans have debated and at times shed blood over just what the Founders intended and how to realize those ideals. A definitive answer to that question is elusive when, as Gordon Wood explained, "the purposes of men, especially in a revolution, are so numerous, so varied, and so contradictory that their complex interaction produces results that no one intended or could even foresee. . . . Men act not simply in response to some kind of objective reality but to the meaning they give to that reality."[1] Meanings are shaped by each individual's interests, hopes, fears, and prejudices, bolstered by any information and ideals that can help justify one's subsequent choices.

In 1775 America was a mosaic of groups differentiated by interests, values, region, class, ethnicity, race, wealth, education, gender, and so on. From that mosaic emerged a revolutionary class that fought and won a war of independence from Britain and created an enduring liberal democratic political system.

Some scholars argue that those revolutionaries shared a common background and outlook.[2] They were largely wealthy, learned, secular, and moderate, and they were united in fighting for a republic or a government in which citizens enjoyed representation and rights. Ideally, a republic at once shaped and reflected the virtue of the people whom it represented.

Others insist that those who led the revolution differed over what they were fighting for.[3] The word "republic" meant different things to different leaders, with some championing a classic version and others a more modern version. As important as the split within the elite was the split between the elite and the masses. The lower orders fought against the political, economic, and social privileges of the elite on both sides of the Atlantic and demanded a more equitable distribution of wealth and power.

Actually, those scholarly differences are not as great as some have made them out to be. The "consensus view" tends to exaggerate the common outlook among Americans of that era, while the "conflict view" exaggerates their differences.

Obviously, each revolutionary leader had his own outlook, and that outlook often changed with time. Likewise, different groups had their own distinct values and interests, which they asserted in the political marketplace. How well a group did depended on how skilled it was in asserting its power relative to that of its rivals. That is the essence of politics. Finally, there were regional differences, while each colony and later state had its own distinct history. Yet the similarities in institutions, values, and interests across first the colonies and then the states far outweighed the differences. The federal government reflected the revolutions that had been occurring among the states.

Class differences among the revolutionaries were nowhere more evident than in the ports, where the small, rich elite; the comfortable middling sorts; and the struggling poor jostled in the crowded streets and lived in close proximity. Ironically, urban mobs composed mostly of society's lowest stratum led the revolution's first stage. For a decade before the exchange of gunfire on Lexington Green, toughs from the docks and the slums burned tax officials in effigy, pillaged their homes, or tarred and feathered them; taunted redcoats and officials and brawled with them in taverns and back alleys; torched a Royal Revenue schooner in Narragansett Bay; and swarmed aboard three vessels and dumped their cargoes of tea into Boston Harbor. This mob violence was not spontaneous but was mostly led by literate and bright men who often penned broadsheets and pamphlets. Yet most Americans were moderates who urged the radicals to restrain themselves and seek constructive reform, rather than destruction.

King George, his cabinet, and most members of Parliament reacted to the radicals, rather than to the moderates. The succession of tough measures between 1765 and 1775, climaxing with the battles of Lexington and Concord, radicalized the moderates. From then on, they would lead a republican revolution that emphasized building up rather than tearing down. That partly involved channeling and sublimating the urban mobs into constructive enterprises; those who had so gleefully pillaged and burned would be pressed into serving as soldiers, sailors, and laborers.

That revolution eventually succeeded because it was rooted in America's common values and identity, or culture. John Adams famously recalled that the revolution took place first in the hearts and minds of the people and only then in armed rebellion for independence from Britain.[4] American culture emerged and developed during the century and a half from when the first settlers stumbled ashore at Jamestown in 1607 and the shots were fired on Lexington Green in 1775. From the beginning, the colonists married old notions of English rights with unprecedented freedoms to own land, start businesses, and have a voice in local public matters. They increasingly saw themselves and were treated by their cousins three thousand miles across the ocean as a people apart, as Americans.

On that foundation, they built a system in which power was distributed and shared in a way that prevented any one holder from dominating and forced all holders to work with one another. That matrix of power involved an horizontal distribution among the legislative, executive, and judicial branches of the federal government; a vertical distribution among the federal, state, and local levels of government; and the embrace and penetration of each of those holders by interest groups, the press, and concerned individual citizens.

Ultimately, the system worked only as far as "the People" fulfilled their duty to help run it. Here again, the Founders sought a balance, in this case between an emotional attachment and a skeptical distance among each citizen toward the system that represented him or her. Hamilton explained what the framers had in mind. Shallow and deep patriotism are distinct, with the former fueled by a mindless emotionalism and the latter by a true love of country expressed by the powerful morphing of reason and feelings: "True honor is a rational thing [that] . . . cannot be wounded by consulting moderation. . . . The ravings of anger and pride" must not be "mistaken for the suggestions of honor. . . . How afflicting, that imposture and fraud should be so often able to assume with success the garb of patriotism, and that this sublime virtue should be so frequently discredited by the usurpation and abuse of its name!"[5] A lack of patriotism was a greater challenge to America's revolutionaries than was excessive patriotism. The new government created by the Constitution would not survive, let alone flourish, unless the framers somehow nurtured a cultural revolution. Many people still believed that one's state was one's nation, that one was, say, a Virginian or a Pennsylvanian first and an American second. The American nationalists strove to reverse that order. To do so, they reached deep into American culture and displayed values that they all shared.

Politically, what is important is not whether a belief is true, but whether it inspires and guides behavior. From virtually the beginning, most Americans fervently agreed with Massachusetts governor John Winthrop, who declared as early as 1635 that the new world they were creating would be "a shining city on a hill," a citadel of liberty, reason, and opportunity, and thus a beacon of hope and an example to those less privileged elsewhere around the world.

That notion of having a liberal culture whose values are at once exceptional and universal is perhaps the core of American culture. Few have better expressed American exceptionalism than Thomas Jefferson, who insisted that "we are acting under obligations not confined to the limits of our own society. It is impossible not to be sensible that we are acting for all mankind; that circumstances denied to others, but indulged to us, have imposed on us the duty of proving what is the degree of freedom and self-government in which a society may venture to leave its individual members."[6]

The belief that one's nation was superior to all others conferred duties, as well as privileges. In his second inaugural address, Jefferson asserted that national interests and moral imperatives were inseparable: "We are firmly convinced and we act on the conviction that with nations, as with individuals, our interests soundly calculated, will ever be found inseparable from our moral duties."[7]

If a revolution is characterized as rapid, systematic change, then the American Revolution ended with the Constitution's ratification. And ever since then, Americans have struggled and at times fought over just who "We the People" are, the nature of their rights, and the duties and powers of the government created in their name.

Abbreviations

AHA	American History Association
AHR	American History Review
ASPCN	American State Papers, Commerce and Navigation
ASPFR	American State Papers
ASPMA	American State Papers, Military Affairs
ASPMisc	American State Papers: Miscellaneous
ASPNA	American State Papers, Naval Affairs
Annals	Annals of the Congress of the United States
PRO FO	Public Record Office Foreign Office
LC	Library of Congress
MVHR	Mississippi Valley History Review
WMQ	William and Mary Quarterly

Notes

Introduction

1. For some leading books on the American Revolution, see Bernard Bailyn, *The Ideological Origins of the American Revolution* (Cambridge, MA: Harvard University Press, 1967); Page Smith, *A New Age Now Begins: A People's History of the American Revolution*, vols. 1 and 2 (New York: Penguin, 1976); Ian R. Christie and Benjamin W. Labaree, *Empire or Independence, 1760–1776* (New York: W. W. Norton, 1976); Robert Middlekauf, *The Glorious Cause: The American Revolution, 1763–1789* (New York: Oxford University Press, 1982); Gordon Wood, *The Radicalism of the American Revolution* (New York: Vintage Books, 1991); and Joseph Ellis, *American Creation* (New York: Vintage Books, 2007).

2. George Washington to Henry Laurens, November 18, 1778, Washington Writings, 13:254–57.

3. William Nester, *International Relations in the 21st Century* (Belmont, CA: Wadsworth, 2000), chap. 5.

4. John Jay to president of Congress, November 6, 1780, in Francis Wharton, ed., *The Revolutionary Diplomatic Correspondence of the United States*, vol. 4 of 6 vols. (Washington, DC: Government Printing Office, 1889), 112–50; and Adams Works, 3:316.

5. Washington's Farewell Address, September 19, 1796, Washington Writings, 25:214–38; Burton J. Kaufman, ed., *Washington's Farewell Address: The View from the 20th Century* (Chicago: Quadrangle Books, 1969); Arthur A. Markowitz, "Washington's Farewell and the Historians: A Critical Review," *Pennsylvania Magazine of History and Biography* 94 (April 1970): 173–91.

6. George Washington to Burwell Burnett, June 19, 1775; and George Washington to John Barrister, April 21, 1778, in W. W. Abbott, Dorothy Twohig, and Philander D. Chase, eds., *The Papers of George Washington, Revolutionary War Series* (Charlottesville: University of Virginia Press, 1985), 1:19–20; 13:577.

7. Daniel Boorstein, *The Americans: The Colonial Experience* (New York: Penguin, 1958); Richard Walsh, *The Mind and Spirit of Early America* (New York: Appleton-Century-Crofts, 1969); Kenneth Silverman, *A Cultural History of the American Revolution* (New York: Thomas Crowell Company, 1976); Everett Emerson, ed., *American Literature, 1764–1789: The Revolutionary Years* (Madison: University of Wisconsin Press, 1977); A. Owen Aldridge, *Early American Literature: A Comparative Approach* (Princeton, NJ: Princeton University Press, 1982); and Richard L. Bushman, *The Refinement of America: Persons, Houses, Cities* (New York: Vintage Books, 1992).

8. Douglas Leach, *Roots of Conflict: British Armed Forces and Colonial America, 1677–1763* (Lincoln: University of Nebraska Press, 1989); and Ian K. Steele, *Warpaths: Invasions of North America* (New York: Oxford University Press, 1995).

9. William Nester, *The Great Frontier War: Britain, France, and the Struggle for North America, 1607–1775* (Westport, CT: Praeger, 2000); William Nester, *The First Global War: Britain, France, and the Fate of North America* (Westport, CT: Praeger, 2000); and William Nester, *Haughty Conquerors: Amherst and the Great Indian Uprising of 1763* (Westport, CT: Praeger, 2001).

Part 1

1. For good overviews of the challenges the British faced, see John R. Alden, *The History of the American Revolution: Britain and the Loss of the Thirteen Colonies* (New York: Macdonald, 1969); K. Perry, *British Politics and the American Revolution* (New York: Palgrave Macmillan, 1990); Don Cook, *The Long Fuse: How England Lost the American Colonies, 1760–1785* (New York: Atlantic Monthly Press, 1996); H. T. Dickinson, ed., *Britain and the American Revolution* (New York: Addison Wesley Longman, 1998); Michael Pearson, *Those Damned Rebels: The American Revolution Seen through British Eyes* (New York: Da Capo, 2000); and Robert Harvey, *A Few Bloody Noses: The Realities and Mythologies of the American Revolution* (New York: Overlook Books, 2002).

2. For good overviews of the politics and the military dimensions of the war's first campaign, see David Hackett Fisher, *Paul Revere's Ride* (New York: Oxford University Press, 1995); and Arthur Fourtellot, *Lexington and Concord: The Beginning of the War of the American Revolution* (New York: W. W. Norton, 2000).

3. Page Smith, *A New Age Now Begins: A People's History of the American Revolution*, vol. 1 of 2 vols. (New York: Penguin, 1976), 488–89.

4. Willard Sterne Randall, *Benedict Arnold: Patriot and Traitor* (New York: Dorset Press, 1990); and James Kirby Martin, *Benedict Arnold: Revolutionary Hero, An American Warrior Reconsidered* (New York: New York University Press, 1997).

5. Page Smith, *The Shaping of America: A People's History of the Young Republic* (New York: Penguin, 1980), 1:532–33.

6. Samuel Chase to John Adams, January 12, 1776, Adams Papers, 4:400.

7. *Congress Journals*, 3:392.

8. French National Archives, AAECP Angleterre, 515:389–92.

9. Vergennes, "Considerations," in Henri Donoil, ed., *Histoire de la Participation de la France a l'Establissement des Etats-Unisd'Amerique: Correspondance Diplomatique et Documents*, vol. 1 of 5 vols. (Paris: Imprimerie Nationale, 1876–99), 273–78; and Joseph Mathias. Gerard de Rayneval, "Reflexions," April 1776, Donoil, Correspondance Diplomatique, French National Archives, 1:243–49.

10. Brian N. Morton and Donald C. Spinelli, eds., *Beaumarchais Correspondence*, vol. 2 of 4 vols. (Paris: A.-G. Nizet, 1969–), 150–55, 171–76.

11. Leonard W. Larabee and William B. Willcox et al., eds., *The Papers of Benjamin Franklin*, 24 vols. (New Haven, CT: Yale University Press, 1959–), 22:354, 369–74.

12. Henri Donoil, ed., *Histoire de la Participation de la France al'Etablissement des Etats-Unis d'Amerique*, vol. 1 of 5 vols. (Paris: Imprimerie Nationales, 1880–92), 384, 402–19; and Beaumarchais to Aranda, October 10, 1776, Beaumarchais Correspondence, French National Archives.

13. Michael Foot and Isaac Kramnick, eds., *The Thomas Paine Reader* (New York: Penguin Books, 1987).

14. Smith, *A New Age Now Begins*, vol. 1, 682.

15. For the best account, see Pauline Maier, *American Scripture: Making the Declaration of Independence* (New York: Vintage, 1998); See also Gary Wills, *Inventing America: Jefferson's Declaration of Independence* (Boston: Houghton Mifflin, 1978); and Scott Douglas Gerber, *To Secure These Rights: The Declaration of Independence and Constitutional Interpretation* (New York: New York University Press, 1995).

16. Barnet Schecter, *The Battle for New York* (New York: Walker, 2002).

17. Smith, *A New Age Now Begins*, vol. 1, 742.

18. Ibid., vol. 1, 756–57.

19. Ibid., vol. 1, 821–22.

20. "Plan of Treaties as Adopted," September 17, 1776, Adams Papers, 4:292; William C. Stinchcombe, "John Adams and the Model Treaty," in Lawrence S. Kaplan, ed., *The American Revolution and "A Candid World"* (Kent, OH: Kent State University Press, 1977), 69–74; and *Congress Journals*, 5:813–17, 827; 884, 6:897.

21. Instructions to commissioners, September 24, 1776, *The Papers of Benjamin Franklin*, 24 vols. (New Haven, CT: Yale University Press, 1959–), 22:624–30.

22. Jonathan Dull, *Franklin the Diplomat: The French Mission* (Philadelphia: American Philosophical Society, 1982), 77, 83–84.

23. Instructions, December 1776, *Congress Journals*, 6:1057.

24. Claude Van Tyne, "French Aid before the Alliance of 1778," *American History Review* 31 (1925): 37–40.

25. Smith, *A New Age Now Begins*, vol. 2, 963.

26. Ibid., vol. 2, 968.

27. Ibid., vol. 2, 926–28.

28. Gerald Stourz, *Benjamin Franklin and American Foreign Policy* (Chicago: University of Chicago Press, 1969), 140.

29. "Considerations upon the Necessity of France Declaring at Once for the American, Even without the Concurrence of Spain," January 13, 1778, in Edward S. Corwin, *French Policy and the American Alliance of 1778* (Princeton, NJ: Princeton University Press, 1916), 399.

30. "Treaty of Alliance," February 6, 1778, in Hunter Miller, ed., *Treaties and Other International Acts of the United States of America*, vol 2 of 8 vols. (Washington, DC: Government Printing Office, 1931–48), 38.

31. William C. Stinchcombe, *The American Revolution and the French Alliance* (Syracuse, NY: Syracuse University Press, 1969), 15.

32. Jonathan R. Dull, "France and the American Revolution Seen as Tragedy," in Ronald Hoffman and Peter J. Albert, eds., *Diplomacy and Revolution: The Franco-American Alliance of 1778* (Charlottesville: University of Virginia Press, 1981), 94.

33. Jonathan Dull, *French Navy and American Independence: A Study of Arms and Diplomacy, 1774–1787* (Princeton, NJ: Princeton University Press, 1975), 84–85; Samuel Flagg Bemis, *Diplomacy of the American Revolution* (Bloomington: Indiana University Press, 1957), 134; and Jonathan Dull, *A Diplomatic History of the American Revolution*, (New Haven, CT: Yale University Press, 1998), 125.

34. John Sullivan to Robert Pigot, April 27, 1778, in Otis G. Hammond, ed., *Letters and Papers of Major General John Sullivan of the Continental Army* (Concord: Collections of the New Hampshire Historical Society,1930–39), 2:40.

35. George Washington to John Washington, June 10, 1778, Washington Writings, 12:43.

36. William Nester, *The Frontier War for American Independence* (Mechanicsburg, PA: Stackpole Books, 2004).

37. Smith, *A New Age Now Begins*, vol. 2, 1262.

38. Vergennes to Gerard, October 26, 1778, Conrad Gerard to Vergennes, October 20, December 22, 1778, January 28, February 17, March 10, 1779, Despatches, 355–62, 433–34, 344–45, 493–95, 529, 579.

39. Conrad Alexander Gerard to president of Congress, February 9, May 22, 1779, in Wharton, ed., *The Revolutionary Diplomatic Correspondence of the United States*, vol. 3 of 6 vols., 39–40, 175–78.

40. *Committee Report*, February 23, 1779; and Instructions to Commissioners, September 26, 1779, *Congress Journals*, 13:239–44, 14:957–60.

41. William Henry Drayton, Memorandum of Conference with the Minister of France, February 15, 1779, Congress Letters, 4:70.

42. Gerard to president to Congress, May 22, 1779, in Wharton, ed., *The Revolutionary Diplomatic Correspondence of the United States*, vol. 3 of 6 vols., 175–78.

43. George Washington to Congress, October 4, in 1778, in Wharton, ed., *The Revolutionary War Diplomatic Correspondence of the United States*, vol. 1 of 6 vols., 360.

44. Instructions to John Jay, September 27, 1779, *Congress Journals*, 15:1118.

45. Bemis, *The Diplomacy of the American Revolution*, 92–93, 106.

46. John Jay to president of Congress, March 3, 1780, Jay Letterbook, New Work Public Library. See also John Jay to Floridablanca, June 9, 19, 22,August 11, 16, 1780; Floridablanca to John Jay, February 28, June 20, July 29, August 12, September 14, 1780; John Jay to president of Congress, March 3, May 26, November 6, 1780; John Jay to Foreign Affairs Committee, May 27, November 30, 1780; and John Jay to Congress, November 6, 1780, Jay Letterbook.

47. John Jay to Vergennes, September 22, 1780, Jay Letterbook.

48. Smith, *A New Age Now Begins*, vol. 2, 1624.

49. Ibid., vol. 2, 1392.

50. Ibid., vol. 2, 1415–16.

51. For an excellent discussion, see Richard B. Morris, *The Peacemakers: The Great Powers and American Independence* (New York: Harper & Row, 1965), 132–72.

52. Morris, *The Peacemakers*, 158–72.

53. Friedrich Edler, *The Dutch Republic and the American Revolution* (Baltimore: Johns Hopkins Press, 1911).

54. John Adams, *Diary and Autobiography* (Cambridge, MA: Harvard University Press, 1961) 2:446.

55. Ibid., 2:243.

56. Benjamin Franklin to Congress, August 9, 1780, Franklin Papers, 23:160–66.

57. Smith, *A New Age Now Begins*, vol. 2, 1431.

58. Ibid., vol. 2, 1457.

59. Ibid., vol. 2, 483–84.

60. Memorandum on conference with Rochambeau, Washington Writings, 20:56.

61. Washington to de Grasse, September 25, 1781, Washington Writings, 23:136–39.

62. Smith, *A New Age Now Begins*, vol. 2, 1708.

Part 2

1. For the best books on the diplomacy leading to the 1783 Treaty of Paris, see Richard B. Morris, *The Peacemakers: The Great Powers and American Independence* (New York: Harper and Row, 1965); and Ronald Hoffman and Peter J. Albert, eds., *Peace and the Peacemakers: The Treaty of 1783* (Charlottesville: University of Virginia Press, 1986).

2. Vergennes to La Luzerne, March 9, 1781, AAECPEU, 15:90; Henri Donoil, Henri, ed., *Histoire de la Participation de la France a l'Etablissement des Etats-Unis d'Amerique*, vol. 4 of 5 vols. (Paris: Imprimerie Nationales, 1880-92), 556; Instructions to John Adams, June 15, 1781, La Luzerne to Vergennes, June 11, November 1, 1781, AAECPEU, 17, 19; and Morris, *The Peacemakers*, 211.

3. Instructions to peace commissioner, June 11, 1781, *Congress Journals*, 20:627.

4. John Adams to president of Congress, June 23, 1781; July 11, 1781; John Adams to Vergennes, July 13, 18, 21, 1781; and Vergennes to John Adams, July 18, 1781, in Francis Wharton, ed., *The Revolutionary Diplomatic Correspondence of the United States*, vol 4. of 6 vols. (Washington, DC: Government Printing Office, 1889), 515, 560, 571–73, 589, 595–96, 589.

5. John Adams to Robert Livingston, September 6, October 31, 1782, in Wharton, ed., *The Revolutionary Diplomatic Correspondence of the United States*, vol. 5 of 6 vols., 838.

6. John Jay to president of Congress, September 20, October 3, 1781, in Wharton, ed., *The Revolutionary Diplomatic Correspondence of the United States*, vol. 4 of 6 vols., 716, 743.

7. Jay draft treaty, September 22, 1781, in Wharton, ed., *The Revolutionary Correspondence of the United States*, 5:760–62.

8. Page Smith, *The Shaping of America: A People's History of the Young Republic* (New York: Penguin, 1980), 1268.

9. Morris, *The Peacemakers*, 251.

10. Van Doren, *Franklin's Autobiographical Writings*, 582–83.

11. Charles R. Ritcheson, "The Earl of Shelburne and the Peace with America, 1782–1783, Vision and Reality," *International History Review* 5 (1983): 322–45.

12. Morris, *The Peacemakers*, 249–51.

13. Benjamin Franklin to Shelburne, April 18, 1782, in Van Doren, *Franklin's Autobiographical Writings*, 519–23.

14. Benjamin Franklin to Samuel Cooper, December 26, 1782, in Alexander De Conde, *Entangling Alliance: Politics and Diplomacy under George Washington* (Durham, NC: Duke University Press, 1958), 3.

15. Van Doren, *Franklin's Autobiographical Writings*, 557.

16. Oswald to Shelburne, July 10, 1782, in John Russell, *Memorials and Correspondence of Charles James Fox*, vol. 4 of 4 vols. (London: R. Bentley, 1853–57), 239–41.

17. Morris, *The Peacemakers*, 308–10.

18. Ibid., 318.

19. Ibid., 343.

20. John Jay to Robert Livingston, November 17, 1782, in De Conde, *Entangling Alliance*, 3.

21. John Fortescue, ed., *The Correspondence of King George the Third from 1760 to December 1783* (London: Cass, 1967) 6:131.

22. Vergennes to Rayneval, December 4, 1782, in Wharton, ed., *The Diplomatic Correspondence of the United States*, vol. 4 of 6 vols., 107.

23. Jonathan Dull, *The French Navy and American Independence: A Study of Arms and Diplomacy, 1774–1787* (Princeton, NJ: Princeton University Press, 1975), 345–50.

24. Howard H. Peckham, ed., *The Toll of Independence: Engagements & Battle Casualties of the American Revolution* (Chicago: University of Chicago Press, 1974), xii; and John Shy, *A People Numerous and Armed: Reflections on the Military Struggle for American Independence* (Ann Arbor: University of Michigan Press, 1990), 249–50.

25. B. R. Mitchell, *Abstract of British Historical Statistics* (Cambridge, UK: Cambridge University Press, 1962), 281.

26. Samuel Flagg Bemis, *The Diplomacy of the American Revolution* (Bloomington: Indiana University Press, 1957), 93; and William C. Stinchcombe, *The American Revolution and the French Alliance* (Syracuse, NY: Syracuse University Press, 1969), 88.

27. Jonathan Dull, "France and the American Revolution," in Ronald Hoffman and Peter J. Albert, eds., *Peace and the Peacemakers: The Treaty of 1783* (Charlottesville: University of Virginia Press, 1986), 97.

28. John Adams to John Jay, May 8, 1895, Adams Works, 8:246; Thomas Jefferson to Archibald Stuart, January 25, 1786, Jefferson Papers, 9:218.

29. Jean Hector St. John de Crevecoeur, *Letters from an American Farmer and Sketches of Eighteenth Century America* (New York: Penguin Books, 1986).

30. John Adams to John Jay, April 13, 1785, Adams Works, 8:235–36.

31. George Washington, "Circular to the States," June 8, 1783.

32. George Washington to Henry Knox, December 26, 1786, Washington Writings, 29:124; and Thomas Jefferson to John Langdon, September 11, 1785, Jefferson Papers, 8:512–13.

33. J. C. A. Stagg, *Mr. Madison's War: Politics, Diplomacy, and Warfare in the Early American Republic, 1783–1830* (Princeton, NJ: Princeton University Press, 1983), 9: 7–12.

34. John Adams to John Jay, August 6, 1785, Adams Works, 8:290–91.

35. Samuel Flagg Bemis, *Jay's Treaty: A Study in Commerce and Diplomacy* (New York: Macmillan, 1923), 46–47.

36. Bemis, *Jay's Treaty*, 21–36.

37. Charles Ritcheson, *Aftermath of Revolution: British Policy toward the United States, 1783–1795* (Dallas, TX: Southern Methodist University Press, 1969), 56, 64.

38. Jerald A. Combs, *The Jay Treaty: Political Battleground of the Founding Fathers* (Berkeley: University of California Press, 1970), 10–12.

39. Stagg, *Mr. Madison's War*, 9–10.

40. George Washington to William Carmichael, June 10, 1785, Washington Writings, 28:161.

41. John Adams to John Jay, February 14, 1788, Adams Works, 8:476.

42. Thomas Jefferson to David Ross, May 7, 1786, Jefferson Papers, 9:468.

43. For a good summaries, see Samuel Flagg Bemis, *Pinckney's Treaty: America's Advantage from Europe's Distress, 1783–1800* (Westport, CT: Praeger, 1960), 1–59; and Alexander De Conde, *This Affair of Louisiana* (New York: Charles Scribners Sons, 1976), chaps. 1 and 2.

44. Bemis, *Pinckney's Treaty*, 62.

45. John Jay to Congress, August 3, 1786, U.S. Continental Congress, *Secret Journal of the Acts and Proceedings of Congress*, vol. 4 of 4 vols. (Boston: Thomas B. Wait, 1820–21), 53–54.

46. Thomas Robson Hay and M. R. Werner, *The Admirable Trumpeter: A Biography of General James Wilkinson* (Garden City, NY: Doubleday, Doran, 1941).

47. George Washington to Benjamin Harrison, October 10, 1784, Washington Writings, 27:475.

48. Combs, *The Jay Treaty*, 73.

49. Thomas Jefferson to John Brown, May 26, 1788, Jefferson Writings, 5:17.

50. Thomas Jefferson to Archibald Stuart, January 25, 1786, Jefferson Papers, 9:218.

51. De Conde, *Entangling Alliance*, 19.

52. Hale and Hale, *Franklin in France*, 2:332.

53. Thomas Jefferson to James Monroe, June 17, 1785, Jefferson Writings, 4:50–51.

54. John Jay to Thomas Jefferson, November 25, 1788, in *Diplomatic Correspondence of the United States of America* (Washington City: Francis Preston Blair, 1833); and Thomas Jefferson to John Jay, February 4, 1789, Jefferson Works, 7:279–82.

55. Ray Irwin, *The Diplomatic Relations of the United States with the Barbary Powers, 1776–1816* (New York: Russell and Russell, 1970), 41.

56. John Adams to Thomas Jefferson, July 3, 1787, Adams Works, 8:406–07.

57. William Smith to John Jay, April 1, 1787, in Wharton, ed., *The Diplomatic Correspondence of the United States*, vol. 3 of 6 vols., 67.

58. Richard Norton Smith, *Patriarch: George Washington and the New American Nation* (Boston: Houghton Mifflin, 1993), 83; and George Washington to James Madison, November 20, 1785, in W. W. Abbot and Dorothy Twohig, eds., *The Papers of George Washington, Colonial Series* (Charlottesville: University of Virginia Press, 1987–), 3:340.

59. As the best primary source for what went on inside the Convention, see Max Farrand, ed., *Records of the Federal Convention* (New Haven, CT: Yale University Press, 1966), 1:381, 299. For good histories, see Catherine Drinker Bowen, *Miracle at Philadelphia: The Story of the Constitutional Convention, May to September 1787* (Boston: Little, Brown, 1966); and Richard Beeman et al., eds., *Beyond Confederation: The Origins of the Constitution and American National Identity* (Chapel Hill: University of North Carolina Press, 1987).

60. "Papers of James McHenry on the Federal Constitution of 1787," *American Historical Review* 11, no. 3 (April 1906): 596–624.

61. Charles W. Hendel, ed., *David Hume's Political Essays* (New York: Library of Liberal Arts, 1953), 157–58.

62. Benjamin F. Wright, ed., *The Federalist: The Famous Papers on the Principles of American Government, Alexander Hamilton, James Madison, John Jay* (New York: Barnes and Noble, 1996), 1:91, 70:452, 10:134.

63. Wright, *Federalist*, 6:111.

64. James Madison to Thomas Jefferson, May 13, 1798, *Madison Papers*, 17:130.

Consequences

1. Gordon S. Wood, "Rhetoric and Reality in the American Revolution," *William and Mary Quarterly*, 3rd ser., vol. 23 (1966): 16, 19.

2. Bernard Bailyn, *The Ideological Origins of the American Revolution* (Cambridge, MA: Harvard University Press, 1967); Gordon Wood, *The Creation of the American Republic, 1776–1787* (Chapel Hill: University of North Carolina Press, 1969); J. G. A. Pocock, *The Machiavellian Moment: Florentine Political Thought and the Atlantic Republican Tradition* (Princeton, NJ: Princeton University Press, 1975); and Gordon Wood, *The Radicalism of the American Revolution* (New York: Vintage, 1991)

3. Jackson Turner Main, *The Social Structure of Revolutionary America* (Princeton, NJ: Princeton University Press, 1965); Gary Nash, *Red, White, and Black: The Peoples of Early America* (Englewood Cliffs, NJ: Prentice Hall, 1974); Gary Nash, *The Urban Crucible: Social Change, Political Consciousness, and the Origins of the American Revolution* (Cambridge, MA: Harvard University Press, 1979); Joyce Appleby, *Liberalism and Republicanism in the Historical Imagination* (Cambridge, MA: Harvard University Press, 1992); and Alfred F. Young, ed., *The American Revolution: Explorations in the History of American Radicalism* (DeKalb, IL: Northern Illinois University Press, 1993).

4. David McCullough, *John Adams* (New York: Simon & Schuster, 2001), 78.

5. Camillus, 1795, *Hamilton Works*, 5:189–91, 6:3–197.

6. Thomas Jefferson to Joseph Priestly, June 19, 1802, *Jefferson Writings*, 8:158–59.

7. Second Inaugural Address, Jefferson Writings, 8:343.

Index

About the Author

Dr. William Nester is a professor in the Department of Government and Politics at St. John's University in New York. He is the author of twenty previous books on different aspects of international relations.